MY VIEW FROM HEAVEN

Sarina Baptista

To my family – John, J.T., Lacey and Anthony.
For the many adventures awaiting us!

TABLE OF CONTENTS

INTRODUCTION

This book is quite different than most books about Heaven. Not many are written by children, let alone children who have "died." I put that word in quotes because if you ask my son J.T., he would say he is definitely not "dead." I have to agree. Even though his body died in March 2007, a most devastating time for me and my family, J.T. would tell you it was the best day of his life.

It wasn't that he hated his life with us, or that he couldn't wait to leave. He was only seven, and didn't really know what he wanted. He would tell you it was because he could go home again. I did not understand this until many months after his passing. Reeling from burying my child, I began a quest to find where he went. I was determined to get the answers to my questions—what happens when we die? Where do we go? Where is my son? Can he hear me? Is he still out there somewhere?

Six months into my journey, I discovered I had a special gift. I could communicate with those who have passed. J.T. led me down the path to meet just the right people at just the right time. As if following breadcrumbs to find my way home, I went step by step toward something, not really understanding where I was going or what I would discover there. Each step led me closer to my son. I could almost hear J.T. exclaim, "Yes! She did it!" each time I found a new piece of the puzzle.

Yes, I did do it. I had a huge incentive—I wanted to talk to my son again.

As soon as I found I had this ability, I began training to improve it, hone it—whatever was necessary to be able to hear my boy. A month into my training, I began receiving messages from other children who had passed. They wanted their parents to know they were all right. I still couldn't have full conversations with J.T., but I was getting closer. I felt him by my side, and knew he was okay even if I only could hear one word at a time.

At some point, it happened. One word turned into a sentence, which turned into a conversation. These were very different conversations than when he was in his seven-year-old body. Along with many other guides, he helped with my training, so many of our talks were about what I needed to do to get to the next level. I cherished our "meetings." I could hear him as clearly as I could hear anyone. I was ecstatic. I had found my son.

J.T. told me where he was and what he was doing. I asked him questions and he answered them the best he could, given my limited frame of reference. Many of the concepts he taught were hard to comprehend, so he would tell me bits and pieces. Eventually, I had enough fragments to make sense of the bigger picture.

To give hope to those who were missing their loved ones, I wrote about losing my son and finding him again in *A Bridge to Healing: J.T.'s Story – A Mother's Grief Journey and Return to Hope,* released in May 2012. In December 2013, *A Bridge to Healing: J.T.'s Story Companion Workbook—A Guide to Connecting to the Other Side* was published. It contained the training I received from J.T., organized in a twenty-four week course.

The workbook hadn't even hit bookstores when J.T. came to me and told me it was time to start the next book. This time *he* would write it. It needed to be from his perspective, he said.

We began writing immediately. He would channel the words to me and I spoke them into a speech recognition program. Aside from this introduction, the postscript and the last chapter which contains questions from my clients, students, bereaved parents, and others, these are J.T.'s words to you.

He reveals what happened when his spirit left his body, what he experienced, who greeted him, and how he felt. He explains "Heaven" and how he got there. He shares why we are here on earth, why we experience life's trials and tribulations, and how to live the life of our dreams. He writes in language anyone can understand, from a seven-year-old standpoint with an ancient wisdom, to answer timeless questions—what is the purpose of life and death? What happens when we die? Where do we go?

Some concepts J.T. introduces in this book may contradict the teachings from your religious background. Please take what resonates with you and leave the rest.

I hope you enjoy this unique perspective from my darling seven-year-old son, who travels about the galaxy and returns to tell his mom of his many adventures. It has made a great difference in how I live my life, and my intention is it does the same for you.

CHAPTER ONE
Light as a Feather

Allow me to introduce myself. My name is Joseph Tracy Baptista. Most people call me J.T.. I came into your world on October 18, 1999. My mom thought she would not be able to have a child, but she didn't remember our agreement. She agreed to be my mom and I agreed to be her son. There was a lot of hesitation on my part; I had been on Earth many times before, and I wasn't sure if I wanted to come back. I told my soul family I would come, though, so I knew I had to follow through with my birth.

My mom had high blood pressure, and the doctors were concerned she had pre-eclampsia. This condition is harmful to mom and baby. It was four weeks before I was due but I decided to come into the world anyway. I chose Cesarean section for my birth. I knew this was the way I needed to be born for my mother's experience as well as my own.

It was a rocky start because my mom didn't know what she needed to do for me because I was four weeks early. I was in the hospital nursery a lot and away from my mom, but we figured it out and I went home to begin my human experience. I loved being with my mom. I loved being by her side when I was sleeping. I loved having her right there. It was the most wonderful feeling.

I didn't know what I was supposed to be doing on Earth because I forgot everything. I forgot my mission. I forgot where I came from. I forgot everything. But I did remember to bring joy and happiness, and

I knew my parents loved me very much. I loved them even more. They would do anything for me, I know. This is how it began.

Two years later my mom was expecting another baby. My sister Lacey was born. It was an abrupt change in the house, for sure. I no longer slept with my mom but with my dad in the other room. It was okay even though I still wanted to sleep with my mom. My new baby sister needed her more, so I was willing to share. Two years after that, my brother Anthony came into the world. He was a big lesson for my parents as he came in with a heart condition and was in the hospital for three and a half weeks. It was hard on all of us, but I was okay because I hung out with friends while my parents were at the hospital with Anthony. They came home at night to be with me and my sister. I knew there was trouble with my brother, but I didn't really understand it. All I knew was my parents were upset and didn't know if my brother would live or die. I didn't know we could choose to stay or go at the time. My brother chose to stay and got better, but he could have left right then. After his heart surgery and recovery, he came home and we were a family. We had so much fun together and I enjoyed every single moment of that human experience. Even those moments when I got upset and my family got upset with me (I was not the easiest child to raise), it was still the perfect home.

In June 2005, we moved from California to Colorado. At first I was afraid, but I decided I would make new friends and that it was going to be a fun adventure. We had a great time in our big house, in our rooms, in the neighborhood, at the parks, and with friends. It was a wonderful experience.

I had an epiphany in March 2007, about three weeks before I was supposed to leave. I realized I needed to take things a little more seriously and help my parents out. I wanted to tell them how much they meant to me, and show them I would be the best son they ever had. I began to behave differently with my mom, dad, sister and brother. I did not know why I was doing it, but, nonetheless, I knew I had to do it. Two weeks before I was supposed to leave, I had a visit in my dreams from an angel. Her name was Hope, and she came to tell me everything was going to be okay. I was going home soon. I didn't know what that meant because I was already home, but I agreed I would go with her. It just felt like I needed to do it. A week before I was supposed to leave with Hope, I got sick. At the time I did not know what "leaving" meant, but I knew I was not feeling well. I wanted to be home with my family, not in the hospital, so I downplayed how I was feeling until the night before my departure. I was scared. I didn't know what was happening to my body, but Hope was there. "Not to worry," she said. "Everything will be fine. Just follow my instructions."

I knew my mom was frightened because I was so sick, but she also knew she was not supposed to take me to the hospital. She knew without my telling her. I thought maybe Hope told her I needed to go home. My mom had been sick that day too, but Hope made sure she was well enough to take care of me that night. My mom stayed with me into the early morning hours. She did everything to help me feel better. I remember she even yelled at the virus to get out of my body. I knew she was terrified even though she wouldn't admit it. She was strong and beautiful. She always was and still is. She kept me calm and comfortable. Neither one of us knew what being so sick meant or how sick I really was. I trusted my mom knew what she was doing. I'm so glad I stayed home in such a loving, warm environment.

But I had to go. In the early morning hours, I tried to rest and my mom was lying beside me in the bed. I realized she needed to leave the room. I didn't know why, but I sent her out. She went to her room to get some sleep thinking I was going to watch television. I knew she couldn't sleep with it on, so I used that as an excuse so she would leave. It was Hope's idea. I was in and out of my body at the time and I listened to Hope because she knew what she was doing.

When I realized I was out of my body and couldn't get back in it anymore, I had a lot of questions. It was as though Hope just gave me answers without me having to ask. She said, "Many of your questions will be answered soon. First, we need to manage what is happening now." All of my questions would be answered in due time. I got excited at that because I always had these questions. I was only seven, but I seemed to know more than other kids my age. I understood a lot about my parents and siblings, but I couldn't express it. My love for them was deep beyond words. *That,* I knew. As I was hovering over my body and checking on my family, I realized I was free. I did not have to be in my body anymore.

I remembered what it was like to not have a body and be able to go wherever, whenever I wanted with a just thought. All I had to do was think it and there I would be. I was so excited. I could zip around wherever I wanted to, but I'd remember my family and would come back because I didn't want to leave them alone. They couldn't see me and didn't understand what was happening. I realized it was going to be very hard for them to deal with my leaving. I was quite sad about this, but Hope was by my side and I knew my family would be okay. I also knew I would be able to help them in ways I didn't realize or know at the time.

My mom woke up just a couple of hours after I told her to leave the room. I saw her get up and knew she was going to check on me. By then, I was already out of my body for good. I tried to comfort her as she looked into my room and found me not breathing. She screamed for my dad and he came up the stairs. My mom was calling 911 and my dad didn't know what to do. She told him to move me to the floor so she could do CPR. The nice lady on the phone told her how. My mom had taken CPR classes, so she got to work. After the first breath she gave my body, a lot of bloody fluids came up. My mom looked at my dad and said "He's dead." My dad yelled at my mom to keep trying. My dad had the phone and the dispatcher stayed on with him until the first policeman arrived. He took over for my mom doing CPR. Soon I could see firemen, paramedics, and more police, all trying to save me.

It was very weird to watch them work on my body. I would call it fascinating. I wasn't scared at all. I knew they needed to try to save me. At the same time, I knew I wasn't going back into that body.

After what seemed like a long time of trying, they got my body on the gurney and took me downstairs into the ambulance. I decided I would wait for my mom, who didn't know the paramedics had left with me.

We drove to the hospital, my mom and I. I didn't care much about my body so I rode with her and she was screaming at me. She wanted me to come back. I kept trying to tell her I can't and it was okay. But she kept screaming. It was hard to watch because I felt her emotions and knew she was very upset. I also knew she wasn't upset at me. It wasn't because I did anything wrong. She was upset because she had no control over what was happening. It was totally out of her hands.

It was out of my hands, too, but she didn't know that. I guess I could have gone back if I wanted to. I could have insisted on going back, but my body wasn't working anymore. I could not have done the things I needed to do. I did not want to lie around without a brain. That was what the doctors said when they were working on me. "We need to get his brain going again. We need to get him back." I went between the rooms where they had my mom and my body. I wanted to stay with my mom, but I was very curious about what they were doing to me in the other room. They had tubes everywhere and were poking me and putting things into my heart. They gave me a shot trying to get it going, trying to get me breathing. It was too late. My body was not going to come back to life.

Looking back, I remember after I sent my mom out of my room in the early morning hours, I felt very strange. I realize now my brain was swelling. It didn't hurt like you might think it would. It just felt weird. My whole body felt weird. It wasn't painful, although it was kind of scary not being able to breathe. Whenever I got scared, Hope was there. I knew it was going to be okay, and I just needed to relax and let things happen as they needed to.

At the hospital, the doctors finally realized I wasn't coming back. I went back to where my mom was and then flew over to my dad who was trying to get to the hospital. He was so worried about me. He didn't know what to do. He was barely coping, not knowing what was happening or what had happened. On the other hand, my mom knew. She knew I was gone. She knew it when she did CPR on me and the blood came up. She knew, but she was really hoping I would come back. My dad did not want to think the worst. He kept asking me to help him and to not leave. It was hard to hear him say that when the decision had already been made.

I went back to the room where my mom got the news I didn't make it. There was a nurse in the room named Paula who had also lost a child. She was comforting my mom and told her it would get better.

I stayed close to my family for the days afterward. I knew they needed me and I was there for whatever I could do. There were many times I know they sensed me because I made a really big deal out of it. My mom wrote about these signs and messages I gave her in her book, *A Bridge to Healing: J.T.'s Story*. I worked hard to help them and I was happy when I could feel some relief from them—when they felt my presence or felt peaceful, and especially when my mom realized there was nothing she did wrong. I wanted to talk to her so badly, but I knew that was going to have to wait until she could hear me, so I worked on getting messages through other people and things.

I remember floating from here to there and I was no longer restricted to a body. It was such a great feeling being able to move like waves on the ocean wherever I wanted to go. I don't know when I realized who I was, that I wasn't just J.T.—I was much more than that and filled with an amazing love and acceptance. I did not feel like a seven-year-old boy anymore. I was this new energy, and it felt beautiful. There were many angels around me, too, and I was grateful for them because I was concerned for my family. At this point, my parents had not told my brother or sister I was gone, and I know it was incredibly painful for them to do this. I wanted to make it all better for my parents so they did not have to tell them, but Hope said I would be able to help my family in other ways and not to worry about this piece of it. I kept my distance when my parents told my brother and sister I was not coming back. They didn't seem to understand. I could tell because they were young and didn't know about death, what it really was. This was especially true for my brother who loved to follow me around and help me with projects. He was three and did not understand my body was no longer a part of me. So I hung around him and my mom, dad and sister.

I also explored other places. I went to different levels of energy within Earth. I visited each one and stayed for a little while exploring. I knew my family needed me, so I was not away for long. I waited until they were asleep to leave again. I was drawn to the other levels of energy and felt I had been there before. They were inside the Earth. It wasn't solid. It was fluid, and not the magma we learned about in science. I floated within this fluid and became totally enveloped in it, like I was part of it. It was very interesting being part of Earth, flowing with many other energies who were doing the same. It was almost like we were on these inner tubes, floating, going up and down. It was not water and did not have waves. We were like ice cubes bobbing up and down. There were lots of other souls in there doing the same thing, almost like an amusement park, flowing, bouncing and hopping around. All of the movement was done by the fluid, not us. We were along for the ride. I learned later many who leave their bodies go to this place. It is like a washing machine for souls, cleansing the life's stuff for those who want it. No one ever told me about it. I just felt the urge to go and found myself there after thinking about it.

It was not like I knew about this place; it just presented itself in my thoughts, and then I was there.

After I did this cleansing, I returned to my house to find lots of people there. I knew my mom, dad, brother and sister were going to be taken care of by these people for the next few days. I also knew it was difficult for my parents because they shouldered most of the pain because my brother and sister didn't understand. I was very happy to see so many people there to help. It made me feel very warm to know they supported my family. As much as I could, I gave my mom and dad hugs and told them it was okay. I was all right. I knew my mom was trying to reach me because she knew enough about the soul to know it wasn't the end for me. She believed the soul lived on after "death" but did not understand much more than that. She had a tough time hearing me in the beginning. Later, I would lead her everywhere I could so she would get information about where I was.

I am getting ahead of myself. The day of the viewing, where everyone came to see me for the last time in that body, I gave my dad a special gift. I surrounded him with this whirling energy of love, peace, and calm. It was just for him, no one else. From that moment I knew even though he was very sad, he would know I was all right and close by. I wasn't about to leave my family. I was amazed at all of the things I could do. I could give hugs, talk to them, and move things around in the house, which I loved to do. I loved to see my mom's reaction when she would find one of my toys not where it was supposed to be. I also loved to give her the smell of my dirty laundry. She didn't like that smell much when I was alive. She would tell me to put my laundry in the hamper over and over again, and I couldn't think of a better way to let her know I was near when she couldn't hear or see me. So I took the smell of my dirty laundry and put it in my bedroom so when she walked in, she would smell me. I loved to do those kinds of things for them because I desperately wanted them to know I was okay.

The day of the funeral I stayed very close to my body and I watched as everyone came into the funeral home. It was a great service, and I felt very loved. All my friends were there. All of those who were supporting my family were there, too. Even people who my family didn't know came and I was so happy about this because it showed me even though we only lived in Colorado for just short of two years, it was our community. We would get through it together. My mom was in a daze and did her best to stand tall and be strong for everyone. I know this was hard for her and my dad. My dad was being very purposeful with everything he did. He had been through this when his mom passed when he was a teenager, and he knew he needed to do it differently this time. Between picking out the casket, choosing music and making the plans for me, my dad and mom stuck together with a strength not many people see in their lifetimes. I knew they would make it. Many couples don't after a situation like this, but I knew my parents would. My dad had always prided himself on teaching me right from wrong, and now it was my turn to teach him about love from beyond. It was a difficult time, and he didn't know what he was going to do. I was with him every step of the way, whispering to him, holding him, giving him information, letting him know I was very close.

I could feel the love everyone had for my family that day. I surrounded all of them with love, also. I would think of love and it would be sent to them. It was that easy. They might not have known it was from me (that would come later), but I sent it anyway. It was one way I could give them just a little bit of relief from the pain.

My parents picked a beautiful spot for my body to be buried. I knew this would be a place where they could come talk to me until they realized I wasn't there anymore and there was no need to go to the cemetery. It was lovely for the time they needed to be there. At the funeral, my mom almost laughed when she was following the hearse to the burial plot. I was pressing on the gas pedal on the hearse to make it go faster, and everyone who walked behind it had to speed up. The driver would realize this and slow down the car so everybody had to slow down. We went like that, speeding up and slowing down, all the way from the mortuary building to the place my body was going to be buried. My mom smiled when she realized how funny it was. It made me happy to know I made her smile.

I stayed near the house after the funeral and the following days. Easter was five days after and I wanted to be sure my family knew I was around. On Easter morning I gave my mom the smell of my dirty laundry for the first time, although she didn't recognize what it was right away. I also had it snow that day because I love snow. It made my family sad because they missed me very much and they knew how much I loved the stuff.

I made it my job to also help my family sleep at night so they could get rest, especially my brother because he was very restless. He kept expecting me to come home and would wake up waiting for me. I wouldn't be there as he expected me to be, of course, so I would calm him down, give him a hug, and then he would go back to sleep. He knew it was me. It was hard for him to understand how I could do this and be all right without a body. Later he would learn how to communicate with me, but at this point, he just needed to be comforted to sleep so my mom and dad could rest. They checked on my brother and sister all night long to make sure they were still breathing. Hope said it was normal for parents to do because they had experienced a huge trauma, but they would be okay.

By this time I had met my Grandma Bernice and Grandpa Roger in Heaven. Grandma Bernice is my dad's mom and Grandpa Roger is my mom's dad. I knew them from before I was born. It was fun hanging out with them because they were family. Hope, my angel, was very close by as well. I knew her before I knew anybody else.

I really wanted my family to know I was okay. I knew they were concerned about where I was, what happened to me, and why I had to leave. So I gave a message to Nancy James to give to my mom. Nancy is Auntie Jen's mom. I call her Auntie Jen even though she is not my blood aunt. Auntie Jen helped my mom when I was born by giving her information about newborn care. She's married to Uncle Rob, who was the best man at my parents' wedding. I met Nancy maybe a couple of times.

I picked her because she was listening. What I mean is she was open to hearing my message. Many people wonder why they don't get messages from their loved ones and others do. It is because you may not be able to listen at the time. It doesn't mean you will never be able to get messages, but for whatever reason at that time, you can't. My mom couldn't because she was hurting so much. She was trying to be open, but it was too painful for her. I went to Nancy and told her I needed to get a message to my mom. Nancy was awesome! She wrote out the message, and I got my mom to call her by putting the thought in my mom's head. She was sitting at her computer and I put the thought in her mind "Someone has the answer to why I left." She pulled out a phone list with names and phone numbers on it, ran her finger down the list and stopped on Nancy's name. Nancy lived in Southern California, and she and my mom weren't close. This was also why I chose Nancy. My mom might not have listened to someone close to her. It had to be someone who she knew, but didn't know well.

As my mom's finger landed on Nancy's name, I told her, "Nancy knows." She did not understand from where this thought came, but it didn't matter as long as she followed my cue. As long as she was open to these impressions, I could lead her to where she needed to go.

My mom called Nancy and asked her why I had to go. Nancy said, "Funny you called because J.T. came to me and he has a message for you. Get a paper and pen. You are going to want to write this down." The message I gave her had three parts:

> *I did not want you to see me leave.*
> *You were the perfect mom. You did everything perfectly.*
> *I had to go. I tried twice before to leave, but I could not leave you. This time I had to go.*

This was exactly what my mom needed to hear. Her questions were "why did he make me leave the room that morning, I should have saved him—why couldn't I save him, and why did he leave?"

I had accomplished my first huge success in getting through to my mom, and I was so happy.

I started to come to my family in dreams at this time too, but many times it didn't work out well. It is hard for us to get into your dream sequences because during these critical times of grief, your subconscious does crazy things. Sometimes, I would manage to get into a dream, but the subconscious would take over and it would become a nightmare, reliving what happened to me or worse. Other times, I would get into the dream sequence just right so it was what is called a "visitation." That was the fun part. I would take them on great adventures and loved letting them know I was very close.

I also loved playing with our dog, Sadie, because she could see me, and I knew she wanted to play. Because my family was very upset about my leaving, they were occupied with other things and weren't playing with her, so I played with her at night. Dogs and cats are very sensitive to spirits when we visit, so maybe your dog isn't really wagging his tail at nothing in the corner. Maybe we are playing with them!

CHAPTER TWO
No Time, No Space

I know my mom didn't hear all of the messages I gave her in the beginning. She dismissed many of them, not really understanding what I was trying to do. She was open to it but it was hard for her to accept I could do these things. In her mind I was still seven and how could a seven-year-old go in someone's house to give them a thought, get inside someone's dream to take them on a journey, move things around in my room like I used to, or do any of the things I had been doing for them? How could that be? I was just a little boy.

Truth is, I'm not. I am a soul. We all are souls and not limited to age.

One of the first important lessons I want you to learn is about time and space. It does not exist where I am. When you leave your body, it does not matter how old you are. You will go back to the beautiful soul energy you were before you came into your body, and with that, you will release all ailments, sickness, and physical problems you had, regardless of your age on Earth. It all goes away when you leave your body. If your loved one had a hard time at the end or was really sick, they aren't anymore. There are some who still hold on to these feelings because they don't know they can release them, but eventually they figure it out. There are many helpers for these newly "reborn" souls, those who leave their bodies and come home to Heaven. If you are worried about your loved one, you can ask for the angels' help. They assist the souls who may have had a particularly harsh time on Earth. The angels help them to remove what we call the "human suit." It's almost like you're wearing a costume and you have to take it off in order to get to the higher places where the energy flows with no time and no space.

I knew as soon as I left my body I was free from my human suit, so I did not hold onto my body at all. I was able to move very quickly through the different levels of energy to where I needed to go. I will explain more about that in a later chapter. Right now, I want to introduce the concept that I am not a seven-year-old anymore; although, I can come as a seven-year-old to my mom when she needs it.

I am no longer limited to the knowledge I had when I was seven. I can access any knowledge I want from any place at any time. This was especially exciting when I was learning about how the Universe works and how to move from place to place. I would think about where I wanted to go and BAM, I was there. I was thinking about being in my mom's room and I would be there. I was thinking about being on the pyramids and I would be there. This was one of the most exciting discoveries I had right after leaving my body.

I was able to explore places with only a thought. I love the caves. There are lots of caves on Earth and each one has a different look. They all have beautiful colors and shining lights. Some haven't even been discovered yet by people on Earth. I was able to find and explore many of these caves. The other places I love to visit are the very tops of the mountains. I spend a lot of time in the Grand Tetons in Wyoming. There is so much incredible and beautiful energy there—it was a place I went to renew my energy if I got tired. Yes, I did get tired in the beginning because I was getting used to my new energy "body," and I didn't know how to get more energy or that I could just create more. I learned quickly when I got tired that I needed to find places to restore myself.

There are so many places we can go to replenish our energy as souls. The tops of the Grand Tetons are where I would recharge because the energy there is very intense. I found little pockets of energy within the mountain and absorbed them. It would refresh me so I could go and do something else. Many on your planet say the energy comes from the quartz, and that is partially true. It's also because of the geometric shapes of the mountain and inside the mountain. If you could take a trip into a mountain, not just the Tetons, you would see so many different things you can't see from the outside of them.

Back to the lesson of this chapter. There is no time or space in our Universe. Because of this, all I had to do was think of a place, and there I was. It was instantaneous. On Earth we put everything into a "time" and "space" perspective, so to grasp the concept of no time and space might take some time. I think of it more like a big ball of energy and everything is happening at once in this big ball of energy. Regardless of how many "pieces" of energy are in the ball, or where those pieces are, they all make up this big ball. I will address this concept more in this book, but I wanted to cover some of it now so you can understand a little more about what I was experiencing.

Approximately a month after I left my body, I knew I could do more to let my family know I was around. That's when I started bringing dragonflies to my mom, and that's also when I moved things around in the house for my family to find. I did it in the beginning, but after a month or so I was able to create more signs and messages because I was learning how to keep my vibration high. I wanted them to know it really was me and not a coincidence. I started talking to my mom, too. She couldn't hear me, but she could feel me and knew I was close. Again, it was one of those things she did not trust. She would say, "Is that really him? No. It can't be." So I had to work harder to get her attention. One of the things I did to convince her it was me was giving her a sensation on her left hip when she was upset and crying. I wanted her to know I was hugging her and that was how I let her know. She could feel me, I know, but couldn't believe it was me. When someone told her I was giving her hugs and could sense it was at hip level, the light bulb went on. I did it at hip level because when I was in my body, I would give her great big hugs and wrap my arms around her hips—I wasn't very tall at the time so that was where my arms ended up. After that, at least she knew I was there when she was crying.

I still had a lot of work to do to get her where I needed her to be so we could work together. It was a start, and I was grateful for that.

I continued to come in my dad's dreams even though he would get upset at first. I would also put thoughts in his mind about me. Many he just passed off as his own thoughts, like he was just thinking about me on his own, but I kept doing it because I knew one day he would look back on all those times I had given him thoughts and know it was me. More importantly, he would know I didn't really leave.

I wanted to be gentle with my brother and sister because they were having a difficult time understanding everything, so I would come and play with Anthony, my brother, at night when he was asleep. For Lacey, my sister, I would hug her in her room and give her all my love because she felt so badly I wasn't there. She was going through many different emotions.

The first couple of months were very difficult for all of us, and I worked hard, as all of your loved ones do to let you know we are close. It is one of the most important things we do from this side, and it is crucial for you because we want you to know death is not the end.

It is said the death of the body is the birth of our soul back home. If you could understand what this means for us, then you would be excited for the completion of our lives. We also understand on Earth it is hard for the human mind to wrap around the idea of no time and space, and what you are experiencing now is just a blip of time. We spend more time out of our bodies than in. In other words, we have more time as souls than in lives. But we make life on Earth feel so real. The pain is so intense when one of us leaves, especially when it is a child who leaves. Those of us in Heaven make it our job to comfort you in whatever way we can. Many times, people don't see the messages or the signs. We understand you may not be open to this concept, and that's okay because we know when you do finally come home, you will understand it. It doesn't stop us from trying hard to let you know we are really still with you.

We are near and want you to heal and feel our love. This is true no matter what we did on Earth or how we left relationships at the time of our passing. We take the love from these relationships and nothing else. Please remember this when you are judging yourself for how we left.

CHAPTER THREE
Leading the Horse

I want to talk about what I did to lead my mom to discovering who she is and what she came to do on Earth. We all have a special job we said we would do once we arrived, and our helpers (loved ones, angels, guides) work hard to keep us on our path so we can complete what we want to accomplish while we are on Earth in this incarnation. We don't usually get very specific about how we are going to do our work because there are many scenarios to get the job done. We do not lay out all of the details before we come into our bodies, but we do say we want to learn certain lessons and finish certain things. Then we allow these lessons to unfold the way they need to. It might be you meet one person who leads you for a certain length of your path, and then you switch to another person who takes you down a different part of the path. Both do their jobs in whatever way you have asked them to do before you came into your body.

The point is that there are many ways to learn your lessons and experience the relationships you want here. It is about free will with the general ideas and lessons you wish to live out. You could have multiple people in your life giving you the same experience because you asked for this to be given as many ways and times as you needed in order to learn it. We carry many of these lessons with us from lifetime to lifetime because we don't quite get it. We keep asking for it to be learned over and over again until we finally understand the lesson and experience the relationship of love with the people in our lives.

For my mother, she said she wanted to help many people remember who they are and what they came to do on Earth. In order to do this, she needed to expand who she was and learn how to do it on her own.

There were other times in my mom's life when she was led down the path where she could have learned about her gifts, but for whatever reason she did not get the full understanding. It took an experience such as losing me to help her realize who she was.

The first piece of the lesson was about her grief and how she walked through it differently than other people. She was deliberate and purposeful, and I was naturally a part of this. I would tell her in her mind ways to process her grief to have the best results. She listened and followed my guidance even though she did not know it was me giving her these thoughts. It was critical for her to move through her grief so she could talk to me and understand who she was and what she was supposed to do with all of this. We worked together so she could reach a new place of acceptance and understanding.

My mom has always been the kind of person to ask questions about why things happen. My passing was no exception. I led her to answers as much as I could, but there was so much she couldn't understand until she was able to communicate with me, which would come later. Regardless, I continued to feed her information so she could see there was a much bigger picture here.

We had a huge breakthrough in her understanding about what happened to me when I led her back to Dr. Brian Weiss. Dr. Weiss is a psychotherapist and a graduate of Columbia University and Yale Medical School. Through therapy with his patients, he discovered they had past lives and many souls come back multiple times to experience life and learn lessons about relationships with other souls. Many years before I left, my mom went to a seminar with Dr. Weiss and discovered some of her past lives. It was pivotal for her to understand we do come back and have lessons. After my passing, I put the thought into her head to look him up. She didn't realize I was leading her to the exact people she needed to discover her purpose on Earth. Dr. Weiss happened to be conducting a seminar in Seattle with psychic medium John Holland. My mom went to Dr. Weiss' website and saw the seminar.

It was not Dr. Weiss I wanted her to notice but John Holland. John had many of the answers she needed, but she had no idea who he was. She didn't know he was the one who would open many doors for her. She said to my dad she wanted to go to Seattle to see Dr. Weiss because she felt he had answers for her. My mom is a very intelligent woman, and she probably knew there was something special about John Holland because her exact words were, "If he is good enough to be doing a seminar with Brian Weiss, then I need to look into who he is."

The next piece of the puzzle was easy to see. On John Holland's website, my mom read he had just published a book called *Power of the Soul*. Now, anyone else who is reading this might think, "Oh, what a coincidence he wrote this book and your mom would be looking at his website." The truth is, this was orchestrated and the timing was Divine. My mom ordered the book and noticed John Holland was going to be in her area a couple of months from then. Another coincidence? It was August 2007 when my mom learned John Holland would be coming to town in just a month's time. She bought tickets, not understanding why she was going, but she knew she had to take my dad and go.

Up to this point my mom had followed all of my instructions, and she was getting closer to the answers. As I have said all along, I wanted her to know I was close by and I was okay. I wanted even more than that; I wanted her to know and remember who she was. I would take her to a certain point and then let her think about the experience, sit with it. Then I would give her a little more and wait for her to understand what was happening. This was how I assisted her for all of those months before she knew she could talk to me and hear my responses.

In July 2007, my family took a trip back to California where our extended family lived—my aunts, uncles, grandparents, etc. Prior to the trip my mom spent a lot of time on the computer researching the afterlife. Funny thing about computers, they are easily manipulated by those of us in Heaven. Especially if we want you to find something in particular, we will make sure it pops up on your screen regardless of what you are searching. It happened my mom was searching past lives and what popped up on her screen was something called a "Life Between Lives" Regression. It led her to Dr. Michael Newton's website. This was the first time she had ever seen this man's work, but it intrigued her because it not only talked about what happened in past lives, but our contracts we agree to prior to coming in.

I had been asking different people to tell my mom she and I agreed to my leaving early. Quite a few people told her this before she found Dr. Newton's website, so when it talked about contracts, she immediately took notice. Of course, this is what I wanted her to discover. She got Dr. Newton's book, *Journey of Souls*[2] and took it with her on the trip to California. As she read in the truck going down the highway, the light bulbs started to go on in her head. I was so happy she could finally understand a bit of where I was and what we agreed to do together. The picture and puzzle were far from being complete because there's a difference between *understanding* you have a contract and *knowing* what that contract is. It was up to me to make sure she experienced the Life Between Lives (LBL) Regression so I could show her what we agreed to "in person," during the regression.

My mom did an internet search and found someone who trained with Dr. Newton was located about an hour from where my family lived in Northern Colorado. She called the number on the website and left a message asking for an appointment. She knew this is what she needed to do to get some answers, and again I was leading her all the way. On the answering machine, the message said there was a six-month wait for appointments, but I cleared the path for her. Within a half hour, Linda Backman's office called back and said there was a cancellation the following week. Needless to say, my mother took the appointment.

Also on the California trip, I communicated a message to my mom through a dear friend of hers. She was our family chiropractor, Monika Buerger, who was just beginning to understand her own gifts. I visited Monika's office frequently during that time to help her with patients. It was so wonderful because she knew I was there and she greeted me every time. I told Monika to tell my mom I had big plans for her. I know my mom was frustrated because she didn't understand what that meant, but to me it was another seed I planted for her so she would continue to move forward and follow my instructions. She was so good at walking forward and listening to where she needed to go.

My mom had no idea that this was only the beginning.

When my family got back to Colorado and my mom had the Life Between Lives regression, I made sure she understood we all agreed to this. During this type of regression, the therapist hypnotizes the client so he or she can access realms they might not be able to reach in an awakened state. As soon as my mom was in that "in between" state, she saw me. I came running to her and gave her a huge hug. We talked for some time and then she asked me her most important question—did we really agree I would die at age seven? I took her back to the place where we were planning our lifetime together and showed her where we all agreed this was the best way to get the job done. It was like she was watching a movie. My dad, sister, brother, my mom and I were sitting around a table discussing what we wanted to learn this time on Earth. We all said this was the fastest way to learn.

I could not show her the entire movie at the time because she wouldn't have been able to understand it. The human brain has only a certain capacity and understanding. If we overload it with too much information that is difficult to understand, then we might disregard some important information we are receiving. For this reason, I gave her the information she needed then, which basically was *yes, we agreed to this.* That was all my mom needed to know. She went home that night and sat in my bedroom. By this time I had become very good at making the mobile hanging from my bedroom ceiling spin so my mom knew I was there. She was quite confused after the LBL regression. She asked, "Was that really you?" She looked up to see my mobile was spinning wildly. Yes, it was me and yes, all of that was true. From that moment forward, she realized there was a lot more to this than just a random virus taking over a little boy's body.

The LBL regression was in August 2007, and by the end of the month, my mother had received the book, *Power of the Soul* by John Holland. She came across a passage about the clairs, which are the senses from which we receive information from the other side. My mom is clairsentient which means she feels things in her body. John Holland wrote if you are clairsentient, it is possible people will mistake you for a store employee as you shop.

My mom had the "A-ha" moment because she had experienced this quite often in stores where people thought she was a store clerk. She had an epiphany. "Oh my God, I think I can do this," meaning, she could be a medium. When my mom met her dear friend, Karen Hawkwood, for lunch that day, she told Karen she understood why I left. Again, the timing was orchestrated so she would read such passage in John's book just before the meeting.

Can you imagine how happy I was when she realized a little bit of her "why" in all this? I knew it was a long haul ahead, but I also knew my mom was up to the task. Following lunch, my mom stopped at a local store. She had a broken toe and had to use one of the motorized carts they have for people who have difficulty walking. She was in the toothpaste aisle, and a lady walked up and asked her where the curlers were. My mom burst into laughter remembering what John Holland had written in his book. She was not an employee tootling around in a motorized shopping cart! You can picture how much I laughed because I got this woman to ask my mother for the curlers. It was all part of the plan, and I was so happy it was finally coming together.

Two days later, my mother had her first reading with a medium. We made sure the medium understood what to say. The medium told my mom she saw a contract and it had very thick ink. The medium listened very intently to me and relayed the message perfectly to my mom—that she was a medium, too—the bridge between the worlds. It was exactly what my mom needed to hear as a validation of discovering who she was.

The next piece of the puzzle was so much fun for me. John Holland was in town, and if you recall, my mom purchased two tickets to his event. This event was a month after she realized she was a medium, and she had already started classes at the Psychic Horizons Center in Boulder, Colorado. She accepted this as her new role, and attended the John Holland event as part of her journey. I have to say, it was very easy to lead her to this. At this event, a local medium opened the show. Not only was this medium a mentor who trained others to be mediums, but she also lost a son. That part was critical for my mom because when a child leaves, parents often don't trust others unless they have had the same experience and can relate to what the parent is going through. I knew it was imperative that whoever trained my mom had to have experienced the same kind of loss. My mom didn't know anything about the medium who was about to change her entire way of thinking and living. That's where I came in. By this time, my mom knew when I was around because I would tickle a certain spot on her head. I made sure she knew I was close by and then I gave the information to the medium on stage to say to the audience.

It was the first time my mom and dad had ever experienced anything like this. It was me, all right, and I made sure they knew it. After the show my mom went to the restroom and ran into the medium. My mom thanked her for bringing me through. The medium told her about how I came to her two days prior and told her exactly where my mom and dad would be sitting and how important it was they receive this message. In two weeks' time the medium was conducting a psychic workshop, the next step of my mother's training to be a medium.

I tell you all of this so you know there are no coincidences. We work diligently to bring messages and send signs to direct you exactly where you need to go. If you don't listen to us, we just keep trying. I was very grateful my mother understood and listened. She knew there were answers out there and she did not give up until she found them. She made my work so much easier.

A note: when you receive messages over and over, it is us, your loved ones and your guides trying to direct or move you. We want you to be successful and do what you came to Earth to do. Listen more and follow our instructions. Let us guide you because we really can see so much more than you. If my mom hadn't followed all of those steps I gave her, it would have taken her a longer time to get her answers and to find me again.

Be open to receive signs and messages from us and you will see how we are guiding you. Many times it is the simple things like my mother experienced—names coming up on a Google search, or something someone says to her, like, "J.T. has big plans for you." We also use bumper stickers, songs, animals, the clouds, birds, coins, and especially other people to bring messages to you. We want you to know how close we are and how much we love you. As you are reading this, tune in to the energy around you because I can guarantee your guides and loved ones are with you right now as you read this. Maybe it's time to stop and say, "Hi!"

CHAPTER FOUR
It's All Energy

Let's talk about what happens to the soul, the spirit after being out of the body for a while. Many people tell my mom their loved ones visited more often right after they left their body, but then the visits became less and less frequent. The reason for this has to do with levels of energy.

I taught my mom this, and she uses this in her training. It is important to know for a number of reasons. First, it will give you a sense of where your loved ones are after they leave their bodies, and it might answer some questions you have about where they are now. As I mentioned before, when I first left my body, I was able to be very close to my mom and my family.

In the beginning, I would come frequently with my Grandpa Roger and Grandma Bernice. Grandpa Roger is my mom's dad. He left in 1995. Grandma Bernice is my dad's mom and she left in 1983. Grandpa Roger loved to be in his body. He loved to have things around him so when he left his body it took him a lot longer to get to the place where I was right after I left my body. He decided he wanted to still be in his home in Moss Beach, California, because he enjoyed the material things from his lifetime. At the time my mom did not realize she was psychic, but she could definitely sense him there. After a while, Grandpa Roger realized he needed to change his energy so he could understand more about what he learned and didn't learn in his incarnation as my grandfather. He decided to raise his vibration. By thinking about it, he moved his energy upward. When we say upward we are not talking about a place. There is no specific place where we are, but in order for you to understand what I am talking about, I will call it "upward." Just by using his thoughts, Grandpa Roger was able to spiral upward to a higher vibration and frequency. Since he still wanted to have material things around him, he created a very big house in that higher vibration space. He still loves his house.

Anybody can create whatever they desire when they are in Heaven. Everything is created through thought. When I first arrived, I spent a lot of time with Grandpa Roger at his house. I don't think it was so much for me as it was for him. I really enjoyed being there, and he and I would visit my mom together. Grandma Bernice would come also so the three of us would visit my family. It was particularly important for my dad to hear from his mom because it had been a long time since she left. He wanted to know she was okay and that she and I were together. That is why the three of us visited my family over those few months. After a while, I knew I had other things I needed to do, so I did not stay at Grandpa Roger's house anymore. This was a little disconcerting to my mom when I came one day without him. She asked about it, and I told her that Grandpa's Roger still wants to stay in his house, but I didn't need it anymore.

This is important because if someone has had a really rough time in life, they might spend more time in that area of space that is closer to the energy of Earth. Again, it's about frequency and vibration. Different people call it different things. Some people call it "tones," "sound," or "frequency." Others call it "vibration." All of these words describe the same thing. Everything in the Universe has a certain frequency and is at a certain tone of frequency. Grandpa Roger enjoyed staying at a certain tone, but I knew I needed to raise mine in order to do the things I needed to do. Especially the things with my mom because she needed to learn how special she was in order to believe what we were supposed to accomplish together. So, I left Grandpa

Roger's house and I raised my tone and vibration. From there, I spiraled upward into a different area of energy.

Getting back to the original point of why it is easier for us to let you know we are present right after we leave our bodies, it's because we are closer to your energy frequency or tone at that time. As we move into different tone areas, we are pulled farther and farther away from Earth's energy. This does not mean we cannot come and visit and do those things we do for you, but it does mean we need to lower our tone to reach you. We do not mind doing this because, again, we love you very much and want to make sure you know we are around. We may not come as often as those first few months after we leave. What you can do to help us is to raise your tone and get closer to where we are. My mom has written two books that describe how to do this. There are plenty of resources if you would like to investigate raising your frequency.

If you can imagine a spiral staircase and climbing it to the next level up, that is what it is like for us out of body to raise our vibration. This just has to do with energy levels and is not a hierarchy or class system. There is no hierarchy where I am. All souls are considered equal. Some have more advancement in their energy than others, but we are all heading towards the same goal which is to understand who we are.

When I first left my body, I was at a certain vibrational tone or frequency. The longer I was out of my body, the higher my frequency and tone became. This wasn't something I consciously did. For me, it just happened. For others, there is a conscious mind effort to raise their tone quickly to get into that space because they remember how to do it. It is instinctual as you leave your body. For some people, when they leave their body they feel they need to stay in the Earthly realm longer because of their family, or maybe, because of the way they chose to leave the world. They may not raise their tone immediately, and that is all right. There are no timelines in Heaven, so it does not matter if you do it right away or if you wait and stay around your family.

Most of us stay very near to our families for at least the first three weeks. What I would do is raise my tone and lower it to visit, and then raise it again to go back into that space of tone or frequency I wanted to be in because I didn't mind lowering my tone to be with my family or anybody else. It was part of what I wanted to do.

It was clear to me when I left my body that my job on Earth was not done. I had a lot more unfinished work with my family, and they also had more to do with me.

For you and your loved ones, it may seem like they are there with you, and suddenly they are gone and don't return for a long time. It might be they have things they want to accomplish in the higher levels, not because they don't love you. We all love you so very much. You can't even imagine how much love we have for you. That is not the question at all, and it is not because of something that did or did not happen while we were in our bodies. It might just be we need to get something done right away. There are many levels in Heaven and so many places to learn and discover. Usually, when souls come back to this home, they spend a lot of time exploring and looking at things very differently than when they were in a body. It is such an altered experience than being in a body. There are no words to describe it, but for this book I am going to use the words you might understand so you can experience this with us.

When you look around your world, what you sense is the physical-ness of the planet. Many on Earth can see into the world I am in now, but usually it takes training and concentration, as well as letting go and opening up. When I want to work with my mom, I lower my tone to meet hers. For special messages, some of us here might combine our energy so we can send a stronger message in your dimension. When we come to your dimension and you can see us (for those who have the ability and training), energy is exchanged between you and us. We do our best to give you the energy so this is possible.

To make it easier, as I have taught my mom, you can raise your tone and frequency to visit with us.

This is how it works. It's like we meet on a bridge, but it is not a physical bridge—it is a bridge between dimensions. There are many layers, which we will go into later. Right now, understand that there are many different levels of energy and dimensions, and they all happen at once. You are a multidimensional energy as you are in a body, and a part of your soul is in Heaven with me. There is always part of you that is in Heaven. You have constant communication with that part of you, and we all work hard to make sure what you want to have happen in life from a soul perspective is achieved. This sometimes means trying to change your current course abruptly. Whenever there is a sudden change in your life, this is your signal that the path in front of you needs to be re-evaluated and, possibly, some big changes in your life are necessary. For my family, I was the catalyst for them to shift and look at what was important to them when my body died.

There are no coincidences, and there is always a plan. What you do with it is up to you. The part of your soul still in Heaven, let's call it your Soul Self, works hard to keep you on course and assist you in doing the work to accomplish tasks in this particular lifetime. If you could see it from our perspective, it would make much more sense to you.

Part of your mission on Earth is to not see it from our perspective, but to work through what you need to without having all of the details. You can always ask your Soul Self any questions. You may not receive the answers you expect, so make sure you want to know the answer before you ask the question. There are also answers your Soul Self and the rest of us here in Heaven cannot give to you, because if you knew the full plan, it would change your course and that is not the point of your work on Earth.

I hope you understand that the purpose of your life, and everyone's is to experience and live it. It is not about rushing through and getting to the end of it with the most success, or the most toys, or the most anything. You don't take any of that with you, anyway. What you do take is the love, the relationships and all of your experiences. When you say, "What's the point?" we answer, the point is to live as fully, joyfully, intently, and wholly as you can. I did that in my short time as J.T., and you can in your current body as much as you want. Don't be afraid of what other people tell you to do, and don't be afraid to do the opposite of what people tell you to do. Most people don't understand what your purpose is, and that is okay, because you do. Maybe you don't feel you understand your purpose at this moment, but within you—deep, deep within you—you do know. All you have to do is get to that space where you do know, and then act on it.

When my mom discovered she was a psychic medium, it took her a long time to be able to tell other people about it because she was afraid of their judgment. She still is, in some regards, but has become so much more comfortable with who she is because she knows she is living in purpose. It doesn't matter if you are a psychic medium, or a plumber, or a motorcycle rider, as long as you are living fully, intently, with joy and wholly, you are in purpose.

Some people have trouble getting there, and that's understandable because we listen too much to other people. We listen to what our parents project onto us, what they want for us, and maybe what they never were. To break out of this and become who you are no matter what that is, no matter who that affects, is a very brave and courageous thing to do.

Accessing your Soul Self is critical to understanding what your mission is, the lessons you said you wanted to learn, and how to get them done most effectively. Again, if you just straight up ask your Soul

Self what you're supposed to do, you probably won't get the answer you were expecting. Basically, what you said you would do on Earth is experience life through certain people and situations. You wanted to have a variety of options so you chose many different people to partake in this life. Some of these people bring you challenges, and some of these people bring you support and love. Some of them bring you both at different points in your life. You agreed to have these experiences and you agreed to accept them. You chose who you are so you could play the game you asked to play prior to coming into your body.

Yes, I said "game." I understand from your perspective it doesn't feel like a game. It feels very real to you and that is okay because that is part of the game, too. The people who bring you challenges have agreed to do this in whatever way feasible. Some of us asked for easier tasks, and some asked for more difficult trials. Within each of these challenges is a lesson—something very important you wanted to experience in your lifetime. I know for some of you this concept might be hard to comprehend because when you look at it from the human perspective, where you are now, you ask yourself, *why would I choose to learn a lesson this way?*

From our perspective, things look different. It does not look so real to us because it isn't real. What we have created with you is what you asked to have in your current reality. Many of you are learning that part of this reality can be shifted so you can have a different experience. This, again, goes back to connecting with your Soul Self energy so you can better understand what exactly it is you want to learn.

Let's say you lost your job. If you were to connect with your Soul Self, he or she might say, "You know what? That job sucked, really. It was not for you. It did nothing for you. You received no energy from it and frankly, it has outgrown its effectiveness in your life." It sounds a bit harsh but probably truthful. Maybe your Soul Self would say something different, like, "I really wanted you to be in a different place right now." Or maybe something like, "I want you to understand you do not need to have a paycheck to feel successful." Or maybe, "You need a lesson about the energy of money, not because you are doing something you shouldn't do but because money does not hold the power you believe it does on your planet."

My mom says to her clients who have "money issues" to not ask for more money because it is a very dense energy. We don't have money here in Heaven. The false power money has on your planet and the relationship you have with it creates cycles we do not wish to encourage. It is controlling, manipulative, and power hungry. What we tell my mom is to ask for abundance—abundance of joy, abundance of energy in whatever form it needs to be, and abundance of life. If you can shift your perspective to ask for abundance instead of more money, you might find money flows easily to you. Your Soul Self might want you to receive money in a different way, therefore shifting you into a totally changed space to allow you to have a different relationship with this energy.

That's an example of what you might have asked to have occur in your lifetime to learn a valuable lesson to bring back to your Soul Self. You'll say, "Hey! Look what I learned, and I finally got it! I finally understand it."

We can spend a lifetime on these lessons and carry them from incarnation to incarnation trying to get the information we need to learn the lesson. It seems funny that we would do this because we have so many other options from which to choose. But it's like that hard math problem in school. You just want to figure out how to get it done. Such is the "math problem" of life and understanding your relationship with money or power, or somebody else's power over you.

The next time you have a challenge in your life, see if you can step out of it and ask your Soul Self, "What did you want me to learn from this?" Look at the person or persons who are giving you the lesson or the challenge. Thank them. I know it sounds crazy especially given some of the troubles you might have, but I'm telling you honestly, the person is doing this because you asked them to.

I have been talking a lot in this chapter about lessons and your Soul Self. I also want to talk about your loved ones who are here in Heaven and how this relates to energy. My mom asked many times when she was learning about how things work here if we can contact anyone in spirit regardless of the number of Earth years they have been gone. She also asked about babies and how they can be contacted. I want to address this early in this book so you understand these concepts.

Whenever we choose a lifetime, we take a part of the energy from the Soul Self and put it into a body. It is a subset of who we are as our Soul Selves. There is a permanent connection between the energy that goes into the body and the Soul Self. When we leave our life and body on Earth, the subset of energy in that lifetime has a permanent imprint from that lifetime. The way I explained it to my mom is that there will always be a "J.T." piece with my Soul Self. When my mom calls to me as J.T., that piece steps forward to talk to her. Now, it's a little different because I am also her guide, so I don't always come to her as the seven-year-old boy I was on Earth. I can come to her as a fellow soul and a wise energy so she knows I am appearing as a guide instead of her son. Both identities are the same energy. This, I want to make clear. It does not matter how I come to her. It is still me, and "me" is defined as J.T. plus my Soul Self. It is the same with your loved ones who are here with me. There will always be that person with whom you can communicate in Heaven. Yes, we do run off and do many different things and yes, some of your loved ones are experiencing other lifetimes, just as you might be experiencing other lifetimes (another concept we will address later). For now, understand you can always access any person who was on Earth at anytime.

Babies have souls, and that soul has a permanent imprint of the lifetime regardless of how many days, weeks, or months they spend in a body. It's the law of energy: energy cannot be destroyed, it can only change form. No matter when a baby leaves an incarnation—before birth, after birth—it does not matter. There is always a soul attached to that incarnation regardless of whether the baby is born or not. So yes, you can access that energy as well. Usually when you connect with a baby, it may not feel like a baby. It probably will feel more like an older soul. This concept confuses some people because they expect someone younger from a young body. Remember, there is no time in Heaven. Souls are ageless.

Another question my mom gets asked regards people from other countries and languages. Souls in Heaven have a Universal language. We speak in thoughts and we don't really use words. We use your words for you because that is how you understand the communication, but where we are, we don't use words. If your loved one did not speak English, it is okay because they will speak to you however you can understand it. There is no language here. It is all about thoughts.

While we are on the subject of souls communicating with you, let's talk about animals. I know for many of you, depending upon your religious beliefs, there may be a misconception that animals do not go to Heaven. I am certainly not saying your beliefs are wrong, but I can tell you that, from my place in Heaven, the energy of animals is very strong. As my mom will tell you, many animals appear to her when she is giving readings to people because pets love their human companions. They come to Earth specifically to enrich and enlighten our lives and bring us joy. If you believe this about your animals, then why wouldn't you believe they would come back to check on you to make sure you are okay when they have to leave?

Animal energy is unique. Animals that come to Earth may choose an animal suit instead of a human one for many reasons. Sometimes, we need animals to help guide us when humans in our lives are not able to do so. Sometimes, animals come to us instead of being in human form so they can experience a different kind of love. When all is said and done, animals are energy and we are energy, so why wouldn't animals have a Heavenly place? As I have been saying, Heaven is really not a place but more of a frequency. There are many animals that have their own dimension or frequency that is not like our Heaven. These are the animals in the wild and some of the domesticated animals. They choose to be in that dimensional space where this energy is created. It is much closer to Earth's frequency, and they are created from the Earth.

All plants, trees, flowers, and other living things on your planet come from Earth energy. This includes many animals. Animals also have contracts, and they know what their path is. What we might view as cruel nature is only those energies playing out their experiences. Our domesticated animals, dogs, cats, etc., usually come from a dimension closer to ours because they interact with us so intently and need to be closer to our vibration. If you look into your dog's eyes, you can see its soul. We all have souls. Every living thing has a soul including Mother Earth, the moon, the planets, and the Sun. Everything in the Universe has an energy that we call "soul."

Energy runs the Universe, and no matter what kind of energy or from where it originates, you can speak to that energy. You have the ability to communicate with the Earth, the trees, the animals, and anybody who has lived in an incarnation or even those who are not incarnating any more. The reason for this is: we are all energy. The entire Universe is energy. Believe you can communicate with any energy, and you will be able to without question. The only thing between you and this connection is your belief in yourself and, maybe, your belief system about where your loved ones, including your animals, have gone after they left their bodies. I encourage you to open your understanding and expand your beliefs so you can realize you have the ability to connect to any of these energies at any time. If you want to practice this connection, I am more than happy to practice with you. I, like my mom, want all of you to remember who you are and the beautiful power and Divine spark within you. Once you acknowledge your potential to connect and believe it and practice it, there is nothing between you and your Infinite possibilities.

CHAPTER FIVE
Earth As We Know It

L et's talk about how we do things "up" in Heaven, so you have an idea of what your loved one might be doing. There are many ways to gain knowledge and understanding. Some of it has to do with our observations of you on Earth and other places in the Universe that provide similar lessons and relationships. I need to say, though, there is no place like Earth in the Universe. There are places we can go to observe how other life forms learn about each other through the experience of incarnation or coming together to love each other, but the best place to observe this in its rawest form is Earth. There is no place like it. We learn a lot from you and what you experience in your lifetimes.

It might seem strange that after we go through the trouble of leaving the planet and our bodies, we still return to see what it's like to be in a body. There are other places and planets we can observe, but most of them are harmonious and do not have the conflict Earth has. Observing the Earth's reaction to all of the energies is a way we learn.

The Earth is a living organism and has a soul. She has agreed to be a part of us who are incarnated, because she wants to help us learn. Unfortunately, so many don't understand the level of commitment the Earth has for us. I am not talking about global warming or recycling or any of these things. Many of you do help the Earth, and we are quite grateful for it, but more than that, the Earth feels through her soul. She feels all of our emotions, strife, successes, and "failures." By the way, none of you have ever failed at anything in your lifetime. "Failure" is a fallacy. There is no failure at all in what you do, no matter who says so or what you think of it.

Getting back to the Earth as a soul, she feels clearly and intensely, and it is often hard for her to hold all of this energy on her own. As souls who are not in bodies, we assist her in holding the energy of the planet. Some of you refer to this as the Planetary Logos, but it goes much deeper than this. We are a collective of energies that support Earth's energy and help her hold everything, including your energy. You are never alone. There is always assistance from us and Earth. I tell you this so you understand that, during every moment of the day, you have a connection to what you refer to as Mother Earth. Part of this connection is vital for all living things on the planet. You would not exist without this connection because you are part of the Earth and she is part of you. This doesn't mean she is the entirety of you. You also have Source (God) energy within you.

Earth has said that for all living things that come to her planet, she will help support their energy. All the trees and flowers and grass, etc., are for your assistance. Wild animals also are part of the Earth and when they leave their incarnation, their energy returns to Mother Earth and becomes part of her soul. It is entirely a system in and of itself, within another system of your solar system, within another system of your galaxy, within another system of the Universe...See where I'm going with this? Many of us are helping Earth and her energy. We also send our energy to all of you through the support of the Earth's soul energy. As we do this, we work hard to assist you to stay on your path and get you where you need to go in order to learn life lessons. It is in the best interest of everybody to succeed since we are all connected to the Earth, Source, and each other.

The work you do on Earth is never a waste because someone as a soul learns from you. Please remember this the next time you think you have messed up and there is no returning from what you have done or are experiencing. Some soul is watching and learning from you. We don't say this to make it sounds as if we are watching you every moment of the day, because that implies we are judging. There is absolutely no judgment in Heaven.

Let me repeat that. There is absolutely no judgment in Heaven. No one here criticizes any other living soul. This is something you can strive for in your own life, to live a life without judgment. Please know, you are never judged from Mother Earth, Source, others here with me, or any energies in other dimensions.

We learn from you. We learn what we may not have learned when we had bodies. We learn about relationships and companionship when under duress. All the challenges in your life are there for a purpose. I'm going to go off track a little bit because I want to explain this to you. No matter what has occurred to you in your current incarnation, your assistants, those who are helping you with the lessons you have asked to learn, might appear in different forms and look as though they do not have your highest good in their heart. The truth is, no matter who is doing what to you, they are fulfilling their role that was set in your plan before you decided to incarnate into your current body.

This is vital to understand because so many of you feel victimized and taken advantage of. It might appear this way from your perspective, but if you were to ask one of us, we would say, "You got the lesson you wanted. Now if you would only learn the lesson and be done with it so you can move on to the next one." One of the things we do is observe how you respond to your lessons and work to assist you in seeing more clearly. This is not an easy task for some of you. You are very attached to how your life is at the current time, and it is hard for you to make the changes your helpers in Heaven and on Earth see for you. We will always work to nudge you toward where you said you wanted to go.

This means that until you learn a lesson, let's say on personal power or speaking your truth, you will continue to get the same lesson from the same or different people. Once you see a pattern, ask yourself, "What am I supposed to learn from this? Am I learning it? What do I need to do to learn it or to remove it from my life?" These seem like simple questions, but the answers are not always clear because you are used to experiencing your life a certain way. Changing the paradigm almost seems impossible.

It is never impossible to make a change, though.

Now, let's talk about how we here in Heaven interact with you on Earth. I've said before, when we leave our bodies we stay very close the Earth's energy so we can give you messages and signs. We use everything available to us to get those to you. Our favorites are music, computers, and other electronics. We like these methods more than others because they are easy to manipulate. I have brought my mother many songs, and I make sure they come at just the right time, when she needs them. I also play with her computer; we have a great time with this game. I can bring my messages more clearly to my mom through this medium. Many of you miss the signs we give you. This is not your fault. You might not be looking for them. It is something you must train yourself to do.

We also are very intent on helping you get through the pain of losing us. We do this by visiting in dreams and putting thoughts into your head. So many times, people don't realize it is their loved ones giving them thoughts because it's something you don't believe we can do. What we do in spirit is communicate through thoughts, as I have said before. We do not use words. It is easy for us to use your thoughts to help you through the pain of grief. It could be a simple memory we give you when you are feeling sad. The memory would be a happy one of when we were with you, or of something funny we did or said.

The grief process is necessary. You must complete it for your human experience. In Heaven, because we have let go of the human part of our experience on Earth, we don't experience grief like you. We do miss many things about our lives, including being with you, but it is a different feeling from the grief experience you have while you are in body. We do understand that part of the human experience is to move through the grief, so we want to help you in any way we can. When I first left, people would tell my mom there is no coming back from losing a child. What they meant is, you never get over it. But I have shown my mom, and she has worked hard to show other parents whose children have passed, that you can have joy back in your life.

Even after a huge loss such as losing a child, you can find yourself and happiness again. My mother is living proof of this. She has worked hard to get to this point. Losing a child is not ever an easy thing to experience, and I know she misses me very much. She laughs now, though, and enjoys life to the fullest. That is the point! We want you to be happy again no matter what happened when we left, how we left, and what you think your part was in our leaving. This is true no matter who leaves—children, husbands, wives, parents, grandparents—it does not matter. We want you to be happy and do extraordinary things to get you to a place of bliss and joy. My mother calls herself one of the blessed ones because she is able to connect with me and give messages from loved ones on the other side to those still on Earth.

Anybody can get a message from their loved one. We want you to know how wonderful we are in our current energy state so you can let go of hang ups you might have because we left.

I have mainly been talking about what we do for you when we leave. This is so important for you to know and understand, which is why I keep talking about it. What you can do to help us is to acknowledge us. Acknowledge we still are there when you feel we are around, when you get a thought from us, when you see something you know we brought to you. Acknowledge it, and let us know you got it. That makes the connection between us solid. It's like a string that goes from your heart to our soul. We are connected.

The next time you hear a song and think of your loved one, acknowledge the message and thank your loved one for doing it. That is one of the most important things you can do for yourself and us.

I have talked before about what we do when we leave our bodies and this is different for many of us, but one thing we all love to do is travel to other places. These other places are within our Universe and since we are pure energy, we can pop in and observe what is happening with only a thought. Let's say I wanted to go to a planet inhabited by all plants and trees and no other life forms. All I would have to do is think of this place and I would be there. Because I am a soul, I do not infringe upon the energy that is there, and I can observe the place without interfering with anything. This is the most fun when we first leave our bodies because we have been confined to a three-dimensional structure and were not able to travel so easily. Some of us go to landmarks on the Earth such as the pyramids, Mount Rushmore, or places that might have had importance to us during our lifetime. We all love to go to other places too, like planets or energy spaces within the Universe.

Anything you can imagine is a creation. Someone created it just by imagining it. This is how Earth was created, by a thought. Each thought built upon the other and we, all of us, created the special place where you reside now. Can imagine what fun it is to create different planets, atmospheres, structures, animals, plants, trees, cloud formations—all created by thoughts?

I enjoy going to planets that contain all water because the energies of the inhabitants there are so crystal clear. It was from these planets we got the idea to create the sea life on Earth. This other planet has all water and only life forms that live in water. When I visit there I swim with the sea life. I can talk to them, and they can talk to me because we are tuned in to the same frequency. Again, it is all about frequency of energy. I learn from them who they are and what their purpose is by stopping by and talking with them. The creatures in our seas on Earth are based upon this model and others in the Universe.

Our current version of Earth is rather new when you look at the entire picture of the cosmos. Many of the life forms on Earth have been inspired by other places in the Universe. These life forms wanted to try living on Earth. They are energy, meaning they are all intelligent and very tuned in to their own frequency and the frequency of others.

Humans were like this too, but things changed.

Earth was created for us to explore existing in a dense energy and co-creating with other life forms. For the earth design, we changed it so that, in our human bodies, we would have free will, the ability to make our own choices, and have our own consequences. In other places in the Universe, the energy flows in such a way that free will is not required because all who reside there agree to certain laws of reality and do not become part of that system if they do not agree with the way things are done.

Earth is different, as you can attest. The souls coming in to Earth now have the mission of getting Earth back on track. At the same time, the energy on the planet has been manipulated, and for many it is hard to see the clear picture of what you were supposed to do because the energies around you are not supporting your path or flow. I will remind you at this point, all of you who are incarnated at this time have agreed to come into your particular life with your circumstances and challenges. You also said you would be able to see clearly regardless of obstacles. This means you said you could do this despite who or what gets in your way. Many of you have forgotten this, and this is why my mom and I are writing this book, so you can remember the original agreement. You have the opportunity to look at what you are doing and make the changes you need to make.

Look around you right now. Who is in your life pulling you away from what you want to do? You have control over what this person is doing by allowing them to continue doing it. No more blaming other people or circumstances for your current situation. Those days are gone; you must step into who you are.

Take this, for example: there are planets where only animals exist. I love to go to these planets because all needs are met. There is no need to kill for food or territory. All energies there coexist regardless of their relationships. The reason I go there is to learn about coexisting with different species and learning to understand differences, so we can bring those aspects to you on Earth. The beautiful thing about the time in which you are living now is many of these energies have come to Earth to assist in getting the planet back on track. You will see two species getting along that would not ordinarily complement each other, living in harmony. It is a beautiful, magical thing. This is happening so everyone can understand we do not need to do things the same way as they have been done on planet Earth. We can change any time. All of the helpers coming now want you to succeed and are assisting in every way they can. The way you can help them is to acknowledge their assistance and thank them for help even if you do not understand who they are or with what they are helping. Just know your helpers come from many places. Their goal is to show you a new way of living.

Another job I have is to explore different energy centers in the Universe where souls are compatible with Earth's energy and ask them to come help on Earth. Many do agree to help. They leave their homes and energy spaces to help Earth with her inhabitants.

I gather these energies to bring them to Earth so they become part of its system, assist in transforming thought, and transmute heavy energies not working anymore. This is usually done on a more global scale, meaning for the entire Earth. There are also many helpers we bring to help individuals such as yourself to understand personal choices and give you what you need from energies in other places so you can feel successful and move toward a brighter energy for Earth.

We are one, after all. The more you understand this, the easier it is to realize your work in all of this. Each of you on the planet at this time has agreed to help us bring the energy of Earth and all of the Universe to a higher place. To do this, you now are able to manifest what you need for your life which will assist others in getting what they need. Thirty or forty years ago when the pioneers of meditation and transcendental mediumship studied ways to reach the higher realms, they discovered much work was needed to be in the higher state of energy and mind before they could manifest. Times have changed, I am happy to say, and connection with the higher realms and other energies in the Universe is easier to achieve. The reason for this is the work all of us have done and all of you have done to bring the frequency and tone of who we are and who the Earth is to a much higher level. Think about a skyscraper with a person on its top floor. From the street it is hard to see that person. If you took the elevator up to a higher floor you might have a better chance to see her. It is all perspective. Since we have all worked hard at getting our tone and frequency to a higher level by following guidance from our helpers and listening to our voice within, we have helped everyone.

It sounds simplistic, doesn't it? Think of a hot air balloon rising up as the hot air is placed in the balloon. There can be people in that balloon and they will rise with the balloon as it lifts off. You are that balloon and you are carrying others with you whether you realize it or not. You get to decide if you want to stay on the ground and not have any movement upward, or if you want to make the effort and lift your balloon off the ground while helping others do the same. Remember, we are all connected, so the higher your tone and frequency, the higher the total tone and frequency will be for the planet.

Your loved ones in Heaven understand this and work to help you increase and raise your frequency so you can live from that higher perspective instead of the ground floor of that skyscraper.

The different ways in which we assist you depend on how you receive information and messages from us. Much of what we do is give you impressions and thoughts to move you into the direction for your highest good. We also put other people on your path to show you which way to go.

Many of us in spirit are also creating new things for your planet. We love to create! All of the amazing things on Earth began with a single thought from one of us. We are all creators and many of us specialize in creating. I will talk more in depth about this in a future chapter but wanted to plant the seed for you so you begin thinking as if you are a creator, because you are.

The next time you have a crazy thought about something to do or create in your life, stop and listen. It is probably one of us helping you understand where you need to go.

Moving forward, let's get into the nitty-gritty of where I am. I have described many things I saw and experienced when I left my body and how I sent messages and signs to my family shortly after I left. A lot has changed now that I've been in Heaven for a while.

To explain this, I need to go back to who I truly am as a soul. I am a high-level soul which means my energy frequency is high, and I have access to much of the information we need to continue to have life on Earth. I say it that way because there are options. There are so many options for us right now because the stream of energy is very different than it ever has been before. Earth has been very far away from where I am for such a long time. This is changing because you all are changing, and we are helping with that change. This next part might be confusing based upon what you learned in school about the origins of the planet. I know for those with whom I work from these higher realms, when I tell them the following pieces of the puzzle, it takes time for the information to resonate with the mind because it is contrary to much of what is taught.

I was one of the frontier energies to assist the planet in its creation. I came from a very different place and was called to assist this new planet, its creation and design. There were many of us who participated in this. It was not just one energy. It was multiple energies from various places. The purpose of this new planet was to experiment with the idea that the mind can create anything it wishes on a physical plane. What we made on Earth was unlike any other place in the Universe, and it became the best place to understand the physical being and who we are when we go into such a realm.

For now, I want to use general terms so you might better understand what we did eons ago. First of all, I want to let everyone reading this book know that you also had a part in the creation of this planet. You would not be reading these words if you did not. What this means is that you have more abilities and understanding of life on Earth than you could possibly imagine. Let's take someone who has lost a child for example. Based upon what we know now about how we come into our bodies with a plan, also called a contract, there is no way any new soul could possibly handle the loss of a child in a lifetime. New souls have to first acclimate to Earth's environment. They have enough on their plate. They would not choose an experience such as this. If you are reading this book, you have chosen to come to Earth this time to learn what you need to learn, which in turn is helping Earth take herself to the next level because you are taking yourself to the next level.

At the time Earth was born, we had many different species living here as subjects. When I say "we," I mean all of us, including you, who participated in this experiment. I say this again because I want you to understand this was not just a couple of energies from other planets who came to create. It was a lot of energies from different planets, places, galaxies, and energetic levels who came together to decide how this was going to work. We needed to see the effects of the planet's vibration on the life forms here. We did not have humans on the planet initially but found the right time to introduce them after many iterations of other species. At first, we did not use the human with the brain we have now. It was a very primitive energy that came into the body. This was also a test to see how long it would take this species to learn new things and to experiment with other life forms on the planet.

When we introduced the mind to the human species, it was a slow process. We did not know what to expect. When we decided different aspects of the human species, we would always test it out initially before rolling it out on a grander scale. The human body is an incredible system, and there is no way this system could have evolved from any species that was on planet Earth at the time. No, this was created with a special mission in mind and was placed on the planet just as other species were placed on the planet.

There is an evolution, but not in the way most people define that word. What was tricky at the time was how this human energy and body with a mind would interact with its surroundings. This was an unknown, unlike all other places in the Universe where certain Universal laws exist.

On Earth, we wanted to create a place of freedom and learning. As we did, we realized some flaws in our creation. The human with a mind will not always make the best decision for his or her path because the human does not have access to all information we have in Heaven and will make decisions based upon only the data at hand. This created chaos on many levels, so we decided to make some changes to the human design. In doing so we knew we would need to separate this human from other species so information could be taken into consideration when making decisions. This, at least, was true in the beginning.

Things change, though, and the evolution of the human occurred quickly. We discovered it learned rapidly and could adjust to its environment and more modifications needed to be made. After many trials, we arrived at a compromise so our experiments, being human, could continue and evolution could progress. Looking back, I certainly do not see how we could have improved the situation any better.

Again, we are working very hard, as you are, to get things back on track. If you haven't guessed, you are a very important part of the plan. Given this information, are you ready for what's next?

CHAPTER SIX
Abundant Choices

Y ou may never have heard much of what I'm about to say. I ask you take into consideration that this may indeed be the way things work. Whenever we are introduced to a new concept, it can take some time for it to be accepted by the brain. So much of what we are taught on Earth is contrary to what we experience when we leave our bodies. We do see a light or a tunnel or something to that effect. From there, different people experience different things which are all part of their reality. I was fortunate to not have an entrenched belief system when I left my body, so it was easy for me to adjust to my new environment.

We all come from a different dimension. I talked about this in the previous chapter. What it means is, when we leave our bodies we do have a choice of whether we want to come back into another lifetime on Earth, hang out a while in Heaven and continue to learn within our system of energy, or go back to our place of origin (more on this later). Our system of energy is often called our soul family, and it means we gather as souls to learn certain lessons in both body and in spirit. We always have the choice to not come back into another lifetime, but it looks like such fun from where we are, we just can't help ourselves. We sign up for another life, or "project" as we call it. Then we rally the troops, our soul family, and they agree it's a great way to spend our time and say, "Think of all the growth and advancement we can accomplish if we do this together."

This is what many of us say to each other as we are preparing to choose another life. We do not come back because of karma. There is no karma, at least not how it is portrayed on Earth, but there is a balance of energy that needs to be maintained. An example might be of a husband who kills his wife in one lifetime because of passionate rage. When he gets back to his spirit self and sees what this action did to everyone involved, including his wife, he knows he must balance the energy. He is not being punished by any means. He is choosing to correct the energy and offset it for his wife and himself. So they both decide to come back and live differently, or they may decide the wife now will kill the husband. This would also occur if there were children involved who needed more experiences with this kind of loss. I know this sounds crazy from your perspective, but whenever there is an act such as this, all parties have agreed to participate. The energy has been balanced and all involved get to experience the hurt differently so they can learn. This is the point—to learn from various perspectives.

Sarina's interjection: *I actually know of a situation where this was the case. A child in my daughter's class was picked up on the first day of school by someone other than his parents. News reports said the father was murdered by the mother. To understand what happened, I asked the spirit of the child's father to talk with me. His words were, "Do not blame (wife's name). She was only doing what we agreed to do." I asked him what that meant and he told me in their last lifetime, he had killed her. The children in this lifetime were her parents and siblings in the previous lifetime. This was the first time I was introduced to such a concept. I was told at the time to not consider it an eye for an eye. It was an experience they all wanted to receive so they could handle things differently this time around.*

We all ask for multiple iterations of experiences so we can learn from them from different angles. You might recall in your lifetime something that occurred more than once and each time you learned something different. Even if it is just to say, "I do not want this in my life anymore." You have made a choice based upon multiple experiences. This is a crucial concept when we talk about lifetimes on Earth. Once you know why you are having an experience, then you can change or move the energy so you can learn what is needed and carry it forward. My mom learned to do this when we told her something needed to be done a certain way. Like an average human, she resisted and said, "No, I am doing it my way." She did it her way and realized it was probably a lot more difficult than if she had done it our way. This is a choice for her, and it is a choice for you. Once my mom figured out that when we brought something to her and asked her to do it a certain way with certain timing, she understood it was for her highest good and followed the instructions. It made it much easier for us to bring what she needed into her life. Even though she has been doing this for a few years now, she still has to remind herself to ask us before she takes action. Some of you would call this Divine assistance and others might call it manipulation. We do not manipulate those who are in bodies, but we do encourage movement in certain directions because of the learning and experiences you asked to receive.

This leads me to the discussion about free will versus destiny or fate. I have heard you talk about how some of you feel your life is planned out for you and you have no options. This is not true. You have many options because when you came into your body, again, you did not specify exactly how you wanted to experience the events in your life, so this is up to you.

Here's an example. You are on your path and you meet someone. You believe he or she is the one for you to marry. We here know this is not the person for your highest good, but he or she certainly will bring lessons and is part of your soul family because no one would have agreed to give these lessons had this not been the case. You go along the path and learn the lessons about your personal power, or standing up for yourself, or getting out of an abusive relationship. What we have shown you in those circumstances is that it is hard to be there. If you are somewhere right now and it's hard to be there, then think about whether or not this is really where you should be.

If you are on path doing what you are supposed to do and being where you are supposed to be, things in your life should be smooth. If you find life is rocky and uncertain, then you are in a learning-lessons phase. Look at this closely and determine what needs to change. You can also ask us, your loved ones, for assistance. Sometimes a lesson is presented to you because you believe you deserve the pain of the lesson. This is just not true. We encourage you to accept that you are so much more than just the person you see in the mirror.

We are talking about two things here. The first is the experience you said you wanted to have when you came into your body in this lifetime and the second is about those lessons you receive because you do not feel you deserve anything better. You could ask us until you are blue in the face to help you out of it, or get on your knees every night and pray for help, but until you accept more for yourself, you will continue to get exactly what you feel you deserve. This is where co-creation and manifesting your thoughts are very important. I cannot stress this enough. Your thoughts become reality. How can you change your thoughts and their patterns to reflect who you truly are? One way is to do some soul searching. This can be done with the help of a licensed therapist who believes in spirituality and the soul. It can also be through self-help methods, as long as they get you where you need to go. You see, the trick with manifesting (as in *The Secret*) is you have to believe you deserve all the wonderful things you are working to manifest. If you do not believe you deserve or are worthy of them, you'll get more of the same junk coming in.

None of this is a bad thing as far as we are concerned because with each of these experiences you are still learning about the human spirit and your self-imposed limitations. Of course, we want more for you. We want you to understand how vital you are to the bigger plan and how connected you are to the Divine and us here in Heaven.

You have more to say about your current situation than you may think. Even though I have mentioned this before, this is a concept worth repeating because it is something we see many of you still not understanding. We really do want what is best for you, as do all of your soul family who is here with me and those with you. Please take time at the end of this chapter to write down some notes on what lessons are coming to you, who is bringing them, and what you think you are supposed to learn. A pattern will emerge. If you do not see a pattern, then ask for it to be shown so you can take your learning experiences to the next level and leave the old ones behind.

Let's talk about judging other people for a moment because it is easy to place judgment on others who have given us lessons and experiences. After reading this chapter, would you agree judging these individuals is probably not the best use of your time? The truth is, there is always a reason why something is being done or a person acts a certain way. You may not understand what the reason is, but it doesn't mean there isn't one.

When we judge others, we are not looking at the bigger picture. We understand you may be angry if someone else was responsible for our passing, and we comfort you when you feel this emotion because we know you miss us. What we do not want is justice in our name. We know this is a very large task because you feel we were cheated. We're not saying you must forgive them because this will come naturally over time, but we are asking for you to not *judge* them. There's a difference between judging and forgiving someone for what they did. Of course, forgiveness would help your spirit achieve what it wants to achieve, but we're not discussing that right now. Throughout this chapter, I have talked about why we do the things we do and make certain choices. Please consider this next time someone does something you feel is against you. You might find this person is actually a close soul family member trying to do you a favor.

CHAPTER SEVEN
"Let There Be Light"

What you may not realize is that there were many times we had to start over with life on Earth. As any good creators, we looked at all angles and did what we could to guide people to where they needed to go. When it came down to it, it was their choice. Unfortunately, when one chooses to go down a certain path, others follow. The Earth got denser and denser as those who inhabited her got farther and farther away from their souls' goals. Our only option was to start over. I don't want to scare anyone. It's not like this was a problem. We called all the souls back, cleared the energy, and restarted. You may have heard of places like Atlantis and Lemuria. Many of you were part of these civilizations.

Aside from a beautiful light being from Heaven and Earth, energy from the Sun and Earth, you are also from other planets and galaxies in the Universe. We all originated from somewhere else and decided to help get Earth going. There are some who are new souls but they are the minority. For those of you reading this book, I can guarantee your origins are not totally of the Earth. That does not mean you are an alien who has taken over somebody's body! That is for the science fiction movies. It means you came to Earth to test out the waters and see what free will feels like since it didn't exist in your original home.

Granted, free will has taken quite a turn. Most people consider free will to be their right. There are very few places in this Universe where free will is allowed to run amok as it has on Earth. There have been many incarnations of this planet and each time we try to make it better. There have been other civilizations who have occupied the

Earth and, for one reason or another, things did not work out. The main root cause for this is free will—it makes humans think of themselves instead of others. This happened in the ancient civilizations where those who had power chose to use it for their own greed. This might sound a little familiar because this is what is happening on planet Earth now.

Maybe you have heard of "star seeds," the Pleiadians, or Sirians, and others who are coming to Earth to assist us. Many people also have discovered they originate in these galaxies through meditation, regressions, or readings. It makes it sound like they are special people because they don't come from Earth.

What I want to emphasize is none of you originated on Earth. The system of incarnation is very complex, but I will try to explain it. As for myself and many others, we came from elsewhere all over the Universe to your Central Sun, and from there we decided we would create a new place for learning lessons about love and people's interactions. There are many places we can observe interaction of souls, but those of you on Earth are very special. You have chosen to go out of the spirit realm and into a body, a very dense body at that. You agreed to forget who you are entirely so you can fully experience the physical-ness of being on planet Earth.

It was not intended that Earth be a place of harshness, though. It evolved into this. As I have said before, we tried to renew it several times and start over. We removed all of the energies at one time, pulled them off the planet. We renewed it using our own energy, and you all lined up once again to create a new civilization. Our hopes were that we would learn from our lessons and would not repeat them lifetime after lifetime. When you go home and out of your body, you will say, as we all do, "Oh my gosh, I can't believe I didn't see that," or "I can't believe I didn't learn that this time around." Many of you carry forward the lessons you did not absorb from other lifetimes in the hopes of learning them and being done with them. Now, many of you in the present are working diligently to eradicate these lessons. Those of us in spirit are very happy about this because each time you do, it removes the lesson from your plan and it raises your vibration to a much higher level.

This does not mean if you don't learn your lessons you cannot advance; you absolutely can. Our work is not complete once we leave our lifetimes. We continue to study who we are and what we are designed to do lifetime to lifetime. You may notice similarities when you do a past life regression as you call it to see what happened in a previous life. You may understand there is a pattern because you said before incarnating you wanted to experience certain things and learn how to overcome others. It is crucial for your soul development to experience life. This does not mean you have to continue coming back into a body to experience this. As I have stated before, in spirit we experience through you as you experience it on your planet.

What is most important to remember about this is you have absolute control over what you are learning and the lessons that come to you. We know it sounds ridiculous because from your perspective it feels very out of control, but as I have said in other chapters, you have control over this.

The original intent for Earth was to be a place of discovery and understanding about the complexities of the mind we created. What it has become is something very different, and the mind wants to take center stage when the soul is the center of all. So we said, "Okay, let's try this out," and many different energies from many places in the Universe came to give their aspects and essences to the new souls who wanted to come to Earth to experience this first hand. Yes, that was you! Many eons ago, you agreed to help and to assist yourself. When you learn something while in a body on Earth, you bring that awareness and education with you to your soul in Heaven and, in turn, to the entire Universe because we are all one. What you may have forgotten is how long it would take to remember who you are and what gifts you take with you to Earth. You work to find and bring them into your life under adverse circumstances. If you go back to the beginning of Earth and visualize many of us sitting around a table with the understanding that we are creating something unique and new, you can imagine how excited we were to begin the project. We jumped in one hundred percent and soon discovered it was a lot harder than what we thought it was going to be. This is why we sent teachers and masters to assist and direct you so you could see a better way of living on your dense planet. If you look back in history, when these amazing masters walked the Earth, it was always when there was question about where Earth was going and what was happening to all of the souls there.

We would never leave you hanging out in the wind without assistance. Assistance comes in many different forms. I just spoke of the masters who gave their great wisdom to all of you, and continue to do so in spirit form. There are also children who right at this very moment are working hard to get messages to their parents and let them know they don't need to do things the same old way anymore. The new children who are coming on to the planet have a much bigger task ahead of them. I know my brother and sister do, as do others. They have chosen to lead Earth into something very different than what it has been. You may have heard about the new Earth, the fifth dimension Earth, or something similar. It is often said these kids are not of this world. Well, they're not. Of course they are not because neither are you.

Is that shocking to learn?

You are also from another place in the Universe as I have said before. Does that surprise you? I know it is difficult to comprehend the enormity of the Universe, but I hope you take a moment now to allow your mind to accept this. I am not saying you need to change your ways just because you learned you are not originally from Earth. The truth is, you have been on Earth so often, so many lifetimes, it has become your home. You choose to continue to incarnate on this planet because you want to learn and you want to experience. What I want to expand is the understanding that you are much more than just your lifetimes on Earth. You are one of the founders of the planet, and you have given everything your soul could give to ensure Earth survives this next change. Because you picked up this book, it means you want information about where I am and where you will be going when you leave your body. You also picked up this book to have a better understanding of who you really are. That is where I come in because I want you to understand how important you are to life on Earth.

When we all decided to create this planet, Earth decided to hold the energy and the Sun decided to provide the foundation and the basis from where our energy originates. We said we would hold our mother and father, Earth and Sun, with love. As technology has evolved, we have forgotten Mother Earth and Father Sun. We forgot we are connected permanently to both. Without one of them, we do not exist. I want to emphasize this because it is critical to your understanding of where Earth is now.

If you knew a long time ago the Earth gave you energy to be born and to be a part of her, would you live differently? This book is not about telling you what you should and should not do. It is about giving you information about who you are and what you are doing here. I do not want this to be a lecture to save Mother Earth or to make you feel badly for not recycling. It is more about your connection to Earth and to the Sun and how you can strengthen who you are as a soul by remembering this connection. Right now, the Earth and the Sun are your family. I am also, as well as all who are here in Heaven and all who are with you on Earth.

With this knowledge, what are you going to change in your life to reflect who you really are?

I want to go back to the statement earlier about others feeling special because they discovered they are star seeds or from other planets. This is not new information and unfortunately some have felt entitled or more special because of this knowledge. It was not the intention when we delivered the information to your planet about your origins. We are hoping that as you see you all are from other places (except for a few of you), you will understand the enormity and expansiveness of your spirit and that of the loved ones who have passed. We are here to help you. It is our job to assist in all you do however we can so you learn, discover, and experience life to the fullest. We want to thank the pioneers, you, who braved the New World and continue to incarnate so all of us can experience soul life completely.

The next question you may have is: where are you from? Maybe you have heard about the people from Sirius and Pleiades? If not, that is okay. This is just the tip of the iceberg. Many have come from all over the Universe. It is truly a melting pot. We all had one objective in mind, which was to create a world where we could learn quickly about the joys and trials of dense energy.

There are many reasons why forming Earth was important to the Universe, but a few stand out among the rest. We love being able to touch and create things. Many of us have created other planets and systems. There are so many of these in the Universe, your human mind would not be able to grasp this idea completely. When your leaders talk about God's creations, really they're talking about all of us including you because we are all creators. This is very important to remember. Just because you went into a body, it does not mean you stopped creating. One of the reasons we made Earth was so we could experience manifesting from within a body. This is not just for a chosen few. This is for everyone. Remember who you are—you are an infinite soul who has chosen to come to Earth to create what you want to experience. Many of you have forgotten you are a co-creator and have turned your lives over to others who seemingly had the power. This is an illusion.

No one has power over you.

So where are you from? Everywhere. Other galaxies, other planets, other star systems. Yes, you call Earth your home right now and you like the planet because of the speed at which you can learn your lessons, but know you also come from something so much greater. What are you supposed to do with this knowledge? Use it! Your loved ones want you to have this information so you can live your life completely and fully knowing there is much more than what you are experiencing in present time. This does not mean you give up and come home because that would defeat the purpose of your mission. You wanted this experience and you believed with all your heart and soul you could accomplish it. We believe you can as well. You are mightier than any army. You are stronger than any hurricane. You have the power of all of the energy on planet Earth to do what you need to do.

I'll get off my soapbox now. We have much more to discover, don't we?

I have not talked much yet about what I am doing now because I wanted to save this until the end. Where I am, there are many facets to our souls, so I cannot say I'm doing just one thing or another. Just as you cannot say you are doing one thing or another. In fact, you are here with me just as you are on Earth. I know I talked about this before, but since we are talking about our souls and what we're doing on Earth, I want to remind you that there is a very large piece of your soul with me in Heaven. When I say "Heaven," I mean in this energetic space. The space is so immense and there is plenty of room for everyone. A very large part of what I'm doing is helping my mom to teach you to connect with us in Heaven.

It is time to put away all of our limiting beliefs and step into who we really are. It is important for you and also for your loved ones here with me. The closer we get to each other, the closer Earth can reach her goal of raising her energetic level to where things are not so difficult for those who live on her. We all work diligently with you so the connection between Heaven and Earth gets stronger and closer. We are ecstatic that you are reading this book and have taken life into your own hands to learn more about where we are, what we're doing, and how you can get to where you need to go.

There's a big piece of the puzzle I would like to share with you now. Let me remind you of a few things. When we leave our bodies, our first job is to make sure our loved ones know how much we love them. We do this by bringing signs and messages. Even if you feel you have never received a sign or message from one of us, I can guarantee we have tried to give one to you. This includes dreams, songs, computer glitches and malfunctions, flashing lights, and electronics going crazy, to name a few. We also give you numbers. If you have seen number sequences then it is probably from us.

After we get to a point where we feel we can raise our tone and vibration, we begin our next job. We check in with our soul family and mentors to see what would be the best use of our energy. Sometimes, we will take time to relax before we begin the next phase of our soul advancement. This is true if we had a rougher experience transitioning out of our bodies or with lessons in that lifetime. It is not that your loved one cannot be reached, but rather that he or she might be relaxing and it takes a little bit more work to get their attention and call their energy in. This usually does not last longer than a couple of months in Earth time, but since we really don't have any time in Heaven, there is no rush to come back out of this relaxed state of energy.

Because we understand who we are after we leave our bodies, we usually want to get to work right away to complete whatever lessons we started to assist us in getting to a higher vibration and frequency. Since there is no hierarchy in Heaven, it does not matter who reaches where first, but we all have an internal drive to learn as much as we can and take that information back to our Creator, that collective energy of which we are all a part.

Some of the jobs we have in Heaven are to oversee or overshadow and give you information necessary to make changes in your life. Overshadow means we come into the physical realm with you and guide you in a certain direction. Some of the greatest inventors, scientists, creative artists, and leaders have been overshadowed by those of us in a high energy space in Heaven. These individual souls asked for our help before entering their incarnations, so sometimes we end up entering that incarnation as well so we can affect some changes necessary for the advancement of Earth and its human inhabitants. These are not "possessions" because it implies we did not have permission to do so. These are not "walk-ins" because the original soul stays in the body. Rather, it is an energy merge. An example of this from my personal experience is with my brother, Anthony. In the beginning after I left my body, I did miss my mom's hugs so Anthony and I agreed I could come every now and then into his body so I could feel my mom. The way I got permission to do this was from Anthony's Soul Self who is with me in Heaven and from others who might be affected by this such as my mom's spirit. There are those on Earth who would tell my mom I was doing this in psychic readings, but what they did not understand was that we all said it was okay. We in Heaven would never do something to harm you or something that was against your free will. This is very important for you to understand.

Maybe you have felt your loved one's presence for a moment in someone else such as a new baby or an animal. We love to see you smile. As long as we have permission, we will continue to visit in this manner. We hope you enjoy those smiles, hugs, jokes and phrases we used to say when you hear them from someone else.

I would like to go back now to the subject of the masters giving their energy to you. I am one of those masters. My expertise is communication. I am also a master creator and work with the fire and air elements. I love to assist all of you who want to stretch beyond who you have been told you are by illuminating limitations and structure as they were given to you from the moment you were born. These confines are not who you are.

There's a lot to understand, but first you must agree there is more than meets the eye on your planet. Science is still behind in its explanations of these things although it is trying to catch up. Don't let that stop you from exploring and creating your truth which may be very different from someone else's truth. Everything you have read so far is true from where I sit. I'm hoping you can see for yourself what resonates for you and what doesn't. You would not be reading this book if you did not have questions that were not being answered. You can call on any of us at any time to ask us what is best for you. We love to assist in all ways.

While we're talking about the masters, let's talk about angels. Angels have been depicted in many ways in scripture, books, and artwork. The truth is, there is no one way to describe an angel. An angel is a very high vibration being who works hard to assist those on Earth and other planets. Earth has been the focus for this energy now since the other planets are waiting for Earth to move upward in vibration so everyone else can move. Angels, as you call them, are really energies created elsewhere who have agreed to come here and provide their energy to those on Earth. I have heard some say angels have never incarnated on Earth in physical form, but that is not true. Many of us have incarnated into bodies at critical times to give the planet the energy she needs to advance. Angels are for everyone. All belief systems, sexes, ages, no discrimination. Why would we do that? We are here to help everyone. If you remember the beginning of this chapter, I talked about how we are from other places. The same is true for angels. Call us whatever feels best to you, and we'll answer no matter what you call us.

What is the difference between an angel and a master? Not much. An angel might be the Soul Self whereas the master might be the incarnation on the planet. Let's take Buddha, for example. Buddha's primary energy comes from the angel you call Gabriel. Others, of course, gave their energy to Buddha. It was a conglomeration and Gabriel's energy was primary. Gabriel also came as Moses' brother, Aaron. It was another critical time, and many of the energies invested in the success of planet Earth came then to assist all of those incarnated. Believe me when I tell you, angels have been in bodies. We had to come—you needed our help!

Other angels go into bodies all the time to help you out of messes. We tell you what you need to hear at just the right time. Since many of you can't hear us in our spirit form, we need to come in human form. We also come in animal form such as your dogs and cats. Suffice it to say, we will do anything we can to assist you and Earth, aside from interfering with your free will, of course.

CHAPTER EIGHT

Where Is Heaven?

There's a lot of talk now about Heaven and where Heaven is located. It depends on your perspective. From mine, Heaven is everywhere, but that's just me. From your standpoint, Heaven is up from you because this is what you were told as a child. The problem with this scenario is it makes Heaven feel far away and you can't get there from where you are. When Jesus walked on Earth, his message was Heaven is on Earth. Through him, by watching him, and following his instruction, you can have Heaven on Earth. Not in the Biblical way as so many have misinterpreted. Jesus' way was in showing you that all of you are children of God, Source, or whatever you call that higher power, and you all have the ability to do what he did on the planet. He could heal others and see them for who they truly were. He did not judge, exclude, and certainly did not say, "You must do it my way or you cannot follow me." So much has been misconstrued, not by anyone's fault. It just happened. Much of what he said and did was misinterpreted by people who wanted to have a firmer structure in life.

From my perspective, structure is human made. We don't need structure in Heaven because we all know what we are doing here. We don't need rules to follow and we certainly don't need other people or energies telling us what to do. It's just not like that. What is here is love, companionship, and an eagerness to learn all there is about who we are without limitations. Limitations are another thing people put on themselves. We don't have them where I am. We say we want to do something, and we do it without worrying about how much it costs, who else is involved, or if there are consequences to our actions. From here, those worries do not matter because we don't do things to infringe upon others. It is a given whatever we do is for everyone's highest good. We understand why you would need to think about these things because there are so many souls on your planet whose agendas are different than yours, so it makes sense. But, just so you know, when you get to Heaven, none of that matters here. What matters is how you learned what you needed to in that lifetime and who you loved, as well as who you didn't love, or in some cases who you hurt to get where you thought you needed to go. This is not about judging you. This is about learning how to do things differently.

We are not "up" from you in the clouds above Earth somewhere; we are beside you. We are not higher than you. I hope you're getting the picture: Heaven is not a place far away from where you are, rather it is a state of energy in which you can live every day. Many of you are doing this now, living in a different place energetically because you have worked so hard at releasing all of the weights holding you down in Earthly terms. Your hard work is paying off, each and every one of you. It does not matter where you live, how much you make, whether you are a male or female, the color of your skin, your background, or who your parents are. What matters is who you are now in this very moment. It also matters where we are in this moment because we are a team and are working together.

Guess where I am right now? Close your eyes and open to me right this very moment because I am beside you. Not what you thought it was going to be? Did you think it was supposed to be complicated? Did you think you had to be special to sense I am with you? All you need is to be open and we can do the rest. Some of you have blocks you put on yourselves or others put on you. There are some who are still putting things on you, and you are allowing it because it's all you know. My mom encounters these people all the time, those who self-limit and judge her for her abilities to talk to me. It seems rather ridiculous to me since all she is trying to do is help them, as well as other mediums and psychics and spiritualists—all of these beautiful souls are trying to help humankind with their mission here. But it's okay because this is part of your world right now. It does not mean it always will be.

Each time someone judges you or puts their limitations on you, it is an opportunity for you to remember what Jesus wants for you, as well as all of the other masters who have come before and after him. You are a Divine soul. You have God's light, the Universal light, within you. It is as simple as that. Nothing you can do in your lifetime would change how we see you as the beautiful soul you are. Yes, we make mistakes when we are in bodies. It's the nature of the game. I said game. It feels so real to all of you, but trust me, it is a game and you get to choose how you play it. Right now, many of you are playing the game as if everything depends on it. It feels real, and the consequences seem huge. You get stuck in the game and can't seem to move no matter what. And you wonder why. We know the answers to this question, and a part of you does, too. It all goes back to the brilliant flame within each of you connecting you to the Heavens which, remember, are right beside you. Getting back in touch with that flame, that internal compass, can make the difference between understanding the game and feeling blindfolded.

The way we see you is as the soul spark you are. This is where all of your answers are. This is Heaven. As you can see, if you can believe in who you are and you have a plan even if you don't know what it is now, you can make anything happen, heal anything, see anything, and create anything with just a thought. Jesus remembered who he was, a soul connected to God. This is how he created Heaven on Earth for himself and those around him. You are just like him. There is no difference between your incarnation and Jesus', despite what you might have learned in your childhood or thereafter. I don't want to imply Jesus' life was ordinary because it was not. He came to teach and to lead us into a new energetic space. These things take time, and it takes longer when humans try to make their own interpretations. It's like the game "telephone" where a person at one end says a phrase and it goes to the next person in the line, then the next...by the time it reaches the last person, the phrase is totally different than it was at the beginning. No judgment, because you are human and learning all the time. This is what makes you special on Earth. But it's time we change the perception and understand how close we are to Heaven right here, right now.

I want you to do a little experiment. Close your eyes and ask for a sign from your helpers. This includes me, since I'm helping you as you are reading this book. Don't try too hard to receive something from us because it is more about us giving it to you than you reaching for it. Do you believe you can receive it? We hope the answer is yes. Do you believe we can give it to you? Of course, we can. We have given you answers before even if you did not know it was us. We are so close to you. What did you receive from us? Did you hear something? Did you see something in your mind? Did you feel something? Did a thought just pop into your head about us? All of these are ways we give you information. There. You just received a message from Heaven.

Now that you know Heaven is all around you, how does that change your view of your world? The way Jesus saw his world was infinite possibility. This is how we want you to see it, too.

You have already opened up yourself by getting this book and reading it. You want to learn and we are happy to help. Maybe you are reading this book because you lost someone close to you. Maybe you want some answers about your own life and where you are going. We are glad you are with us and giving us the chance to answer your questions. We are still learning too, which makes this process helpful for both of us because we want to be able to communicate more effectively with you. Each of you brings something new to us. It's a partnership, and with any partnership there is a learning curve. Be gentle with us and yourself! We are in this together and we will succeed. Your part is to explore who you are as a Heavenly being while living in a body on planet Earth. Do you remember the movie *Contact*[4]?

The main character went through a lot to get to another planet and prove aliens exist, yet she came back with no proof of her trip, other than an eighteen hour recording of static. That's what it's like for you as you embark on this journey to discover who you are and where Heaven is for you. We are here and we let you know in every way possible how close we are to you, but the proof is not absolute.

How do you define "Soul"? Can you put quantitative terms on it? We know quantum physics is working to do this, but still much of the scientific community is not buying it. Individuals like Dr. Eben Alexander, a respected neurosurgeon who catalogs his own near-death experience with incredible detail and absolute medical proof, are criticized, critiqued, and judged for their participation in the idea of life after death that differs from what was taught on Sunday mornings or in medical school. It takes a strong soul to stand in his truth and convictions regardless of fallout from community and so-called experts. You are all experts because you are living in your finite bodies. You have all of the restraint systems, amnesia about who you are, struggling to figure out what it is that makes you special. If you get nothing else from this chapter, I hope you understand how special you are by being exactly who you are. No other credentials are necessary.

Where is Heaven? Heaven is within you and around you. It is not separate from you. It is a part of you and always will be because you come from Heaven, you are Heaven, and Heaven is you. It is not a place. It is energy. Heaven lives within you whether you know it or not.

I spent the first chapter talking about what happened when my body died and my soul rose out of my body, and how I experienced life outside of that body in the first months. At that moment, I knew I became part of the environment I was in. This is different than saying I am a part of a group or a club or anything like that because it implies separateness. That's not how this works. You are *it*. There is no separation.

If you knew as you were standing in line for your latte the person in front of you and the person behind you came from your immediate family, would you treat them differently? Would you have a greater sense of belonging to something bigger? Those of you who live in a small town probably get this concept because everywhere you go you meet people you know. If you were born and raised in a big city, this might be harder for you to visualize. Imagine going to the store, walking in and every single person in that store is a member of your family. Would you act differently knowing everyone around you knows you intimately, or would you act the same as you always act? Wherever you go, those of us in spirit and those of us in bodies are all part of your family. We all come from the same fabric. We are not separate from each other. Your loved ones with me in Heaven understand this and regardless of what they did in their lifetime with you, they get it now. They were able to see everything they did in their lives from everyone's perspective, not just their own. This is huge to understand, and it is a responsibility we carry when we say we are ready to go back into bodies and carry out our missions. As soon as we come into a life on Earth, we forget we are part of Heaven and the connection with everything and everyone around us. We act as though we are separate, and we do things to others with the belief that we are isolated beings. If only you could see it from our heavenly perspective. Understand that everything you do affects everything around you, all over the world, and beyond.

Sometimes it's easier for humans to believe they are separate because then they don't need to take responsibility for their actions, the planet, and its inhabitants. This is an old mindset. Like the stone thrown into the lake creating ripples that flow to the shore, all thoughts and actions create a ripple effect everywhere. We are affected by your choices here in Heaven as well. The changes you make in your plan change the way we learn and respond to you.

This is important because you must take responsibility for all you do.

Let me remind you we are not judging you. God, Source, The One, what you call that higher power, does not judge you. If more of you could reach the knowing that Heaven is within you and everything you touch is part of everyone else's experience, it would help everyone get to the energy space where true connection is a given. Wouldn't it be nice to have Heaven on Earth? You can do this by being mindful of your own thoughts and actions. If you have not gathered by now, you have so much more control and power over your own circumstances than what you may have been led to believe. This means you can change all of the circumstances in your life you do not like, provided these changes are for your highest good and you did not ask for particular lessons to be given to you.

How do you know if it is a lesson for you or if you can change it? Ask, "Is this for my highest good?" Receive the answer, like you did earlier from me and your helpers. Know the answer is within. You do not need any special tools. You already received those tools when you were in Heaven with me, before you came into your body. They are within you. Finding those tools might prove challenging for some. This does not mean you can't find them; it just means you need to look for them a little bit more than on the surface.

"Is this for my highest good?" That is a question you should ask yourself for every action, reaction, thought, intention, or anything else you do because doing everything for your highest good is what will bring you the most energy and the most light. It is also logical that if it is for your highest good, it is also for the highest good of everyone around you—the planet, the Universe, and us. Despite what has transpired earlier in Earth's history, we have great faith in you that you know what is best for you and those around you. We have given you free will. That's what it's all about. Free will. As I said in other chapters, free will has gone awry in many cases. Don't be one of them. Use it to determine what is for your highest good. Then you can be confident in knowing your next step will be the best for you and the situation.

Even though this book is not a training manual, I would like to include some information on how to get clear so you can feel a part of the Universe and get in touch with the Heavenly spark within. If you are new to the spiritual way of living, there are plenty of books that detail how to get clearer in your thoughts and actions. Avoid all materials that claim there is a hierarchy because this is a false truth from our perspective in Heaven. Anything that tells you one way is better than another way or has any judgment implied can be discarded. You will know what is right for you because as you read it you will feel lighter instead of feeling judged or heavy. We have found much of the writings still come from the human position instead of Heaven's perspective. From Heaven, all are equal, all are connected, and all are perfect just as they are. You must remember this no matter what. Staying clear is necessary when you are in a body. Jesus was in a body and you can tell from his personal experience that it wasn't easy. His story is glorified in many ways because the storytellers want to impress upon the reader the importance of the message. Maybe it needed to be done by making the teacher, Jesus, seem more important than his subjects. This was not a wrong approach, but it did not give the message the emphasis that we are all like Jesus.

I've been talking a lot about Jesus in this chapter because when we talk about Heaven, many of us associate this with "God" or "Jesus" or whichever deity we worship. None of these deities are better or more capable than you.

Is that hard for you to believe? If you were raised with any kind of organized religion, what I just wrote there would be considered sacrilege. I hope you understand why I said it the way I did. I want you to know and believe you are Heaven in a body. You have come to Earth to experience this playground and to bring back to all of us what you learned through your experiences and lessons. This is all there is to it. Learn and share.

Even though this is not a spiritual manual, I do want you to write down some things. First of all, what is your name? That's a funny thing to ask, isn't it? The name you are given was chosen to represent you in this incarnation and you are very attached to it. I was attached to "J.T."

when I was there, but now I know it is just part of who I am. Lesson point: you are not just your name. You are so much more.

Next thing to write down, what is it you want from your life now? Don't know where to begin? Start with relationships. How are your relationships in your life now? Are they fulfilling and bringing you what you need? Or do you feel used or bored? Some of these relationships are ones that you have asked to have in your life so you can experience different emotional attachments. Some of them have outlived their usefulness. This does not mean you kick a person to the curb, but it does mean you need to reevaluate what you are gaining from the relationship and what needs to change. If you are not being respected in any of your relationships, something has to shift. It is no longer just about you. It is the things you accept and don't accept that sends ripples through the rest of the Universe. If you do not accept yourself as Heaven on Earth, then you hold yourself back as well as the rest of us.

You are worthy of greatness.

Now, write, how are you at perceiving others' emotions? Are you very sensitive? Do you live in your own world and do not have any attachment to your fellow beings, the rest of humanity? I asked this because there are some very sensitive souls on the planet right now and I will address this group first. You came to Earth to be sensitive and to learn about yourself through others. This does not mean you give away your power or have to take on others' feelings. It means you learn from them. No more. The time is now to remember you have come to learn about people through feelings, but it does not mean you *are* those feelings.

Now let's speak to the group who has no idea what I said in the last paragraph because you are wrapped up in your own stuff and you lost understanding of what's going on around you. No judgment. Just observation. If you cannot see what's happening and respond to your environment, you are missing the point. You will constantly be battling the "who am I?" question because you have no reference.

For those of you who understand what I am saying, I know you know someone who is not connected to the larger world. Please understand they are working on their stuff too, just doing it in a different way. Here is an exercise: go to a coffee shop or restaurant or other public place, sit at a table and tune in to the other occupants. Does this feel comfortable to you? I'm not saying you have to become anyone else other than who you are. If you live on an island energetically, you might have a harder time understanding your connection to everyone around you. Your job is to reengage with those around you energetically. This does not mean you have to start conversations with strangers or invite people you don't know into your home. You can tune in energetically to anyone anytime by asking the soul of that person if it is all right to do so. Feel the connection to those around you and you will start to feel Heaven on Earth.

Many of you reading this book have had emotional wounding in your hearts making it more challenging to open up to others energetically and find that spark within. You were told that spark did not exist, you were not worthy to have all you wanted in life, and there was a foreboding god waiting for you on "judgment day" at Heaven's gate. I am not criticizing those who believe this. I'm saying that where I am it does not exist. You have to decide what is your truth about Heaven and Earth. I hope throughout this chapter I have explained this concept enough. If you do have wounding and find it hard to believe you are Heaven on Earth, do what you need to do to heal in your own way and in your own time.

You are not on the planet to suffer. You are on the planet to learn. For some this feels like it's the same thing, but it is not because suffering implies a never-ending emotional or physical manifestation of pain. At any time during your lessons, you can say, "Okay I get it. Moving on..." and be done with it. This is providing you really do get the lesson. Don't worry about forgetting what you were supposed to learn. You'll get plenty of reminders along the way.

Heaven on Earth is you. I hope you bring this into your heart. Spend each moment of each day knowing how close you are to Heaven and how close we are to you.

CHAPTER NINE
An Eye for an Eye

W e're all so concerned about our bodies and what happens to them when they stop working. From the Heavenly perspective, the body is a vehicle to accomplish what we need to get done. We love our bodies because they provide the means to experience different sensations, but they really are only a vehicle. When we hurt our bodies or get hurt by others, we take it so seriously. From my perspective now, the body is a shell that houses the energy and consciousness we bring in to whatever incarnation we have chosen. When we say we harm our bodies, we really are not harming anything important. This might shock you, but you cannot harm your soul. It is not possible. I bring this up because many of your loved ones had damaged bodies when they left. I want you to understand *they* were not damaged. They are whole and always will be regardless of what happens to the shell.

The other thing with which we concern ourselves is the pain our loved ones may have experienced during their last moments. I can tell you we do not experience the pain. During the last moments, our soul has already exited the body so it is not in pain and has not been harmed. It's important for you to know our bodies in this light because many of you focus on what was happening with our bodies as we passed, whether it was by accident, suicide, drowning, illness, or at someone else's hand. This might be hard to read if your loved one left by someone else's doing, because from your perspective that person should be punished, even killed, for what they did to your loved one.

We understand this emotion, however, it is not the full picture. I'd like to remind you of what I said in earlier chapters about how we choose what we're doing on Earth, our lessons, our interactions with others, and how we want to exit the lifetime we are about to enter. This includes having our life ended at another's hand.

It might sound crazy because we have been led to believe there are bad people on the planet and our mission is a stay away from them. The truth is, I will repeat this, nothing happens to you unless it is supposed to. The same can be said for your loved ones. Yes, the person who took your loved one's life agreed with him or her to be a participant in this interaction. The soul within the perpetrator who took your loved one's life knew it was going to happen and your loved one's soul knew it as well. I'm not saying that just because it was prearranged the pain is minimized, or you need to befriend those who hurt you deeply, but your lesson is to forgive them no matter how hard or impossible this might feel to you.

Your life has purpose, just as your loved one's life has purpose. You are not to spend your life holding anger and un-forgiveness for anyone. It is counter to the mission you chose when you came into this incarnation. The same can be said for those who judge anyone who took another's life.

Our suggestion is to shut off the news and never watch it again. Many of you who are reading this might say to yourself, "Where is the justice? Aren't I supposed to be involved in the world around me? Have compassion for my fellow beings and be an active participant in my world?" Yes, of course, but this can be done without the histrionics of those who wish to keep you emotionally engaged. Many emotions on your planet have a very low vibration. These are the emotions we do not need to exacerbate. There are plenty of others around you who can do this. Your job is to engage with your heart from a place of understanding and knowing about how things operate on your planet and your part in the bigger picture. You do not need to engage in the lower vibration emotions such as guilt, outrage, any rage for that matter, or fear. Fear is a big one and usually has other emotions attached to it. Why we allowed fear on the planet to begin with is a mystery. Actually I know why, because if we didn't have fear, we might not truly understand the opposite of fear which is love.

Much of the planet now is buried in fear and this gets activated when you read the paper or hear the news. This is not a good use of your energy, and your loved ones prefer it if you just don't do it anymore. If you must engage with the world through the media, look for uplifting and positive stories of love, understanding of humanity, and relationships that exemplify the trueness of the heart.

We don't intend you bury your head in the sand, but we do intend you to be mindful about what you bring into your energy field and into your life. You are an advanced soul and don't forget that. How do I know? Because you're reading this book. By picking it up and wanting to know more about Heaven and Earth, you made a choice to create a new truth for yourself. You get to decide what it looks like because it's not the same for everyone. There is a common theme which is shining your light so brightly it wakes up even the sleepiest soul.

If you were to ask my mom what her lessons were for this lifetime, she would give you a long list. The advanced souls ask for the difficult jobs. Remember this when you are beating yourself up or asking, "Why me?" My mom's childhood was not as horrible as many, but it certainly had its challenges and much of what her parents gave her, such as their fear and lack of personal power, have been the exact obstacles she asked to work on in this lifetime. Her father was a probation officer and saw the worst in people. Her mother is very fear based and doesn't even realize it. So when my mom gets the opportunity to face one of her fears or obstacles, she knows she is doing it not only for her but for possible lifetimes ahead of her as well as her children and her past lifetimes.

Here is where it gets interesting. Remember the concept of no time and no space? It might be difficult for human minds to grasp that everything is happening at once. This includes all of our lifetimes and choices. The linear world is only on Earth. If you or my mom learns a lesson or overcomes an obstacle, past and future lifetimes are affected in a positive way. Because of this, it is very important to bring into your space only the energy you want, not the energy that does not suit you, i.e., anyone who takes away your personal power or instills fear in you in any way. This not only affects you in the present but also the future you's, past you's, not to mention your present you. Remember who you are. You are an advanced soul connected permanently to your Soul Self. Would your Soul Self want you to experience life the way you are living it now or would he or she say "I have bigger plans for you. Let's get started!"?

Your loved ones would say they see a beautiful path in front of you with luscious green grass and gorgeous fields of flowers. They would tell you what a bright light you have, how much they love you and want you to have the same affection for yourself as they have for you. They would tell you it's a piece of cake to get where you need to go. It is important to understand the world is a part of you, and you can discard pieces that do not work for you. When I was on Earth, I had many jobs I needed to do in a short time. I got to work right away. One of these jobs was to make as many friends as I could because I knew these friends needed me as much as I needed them. I continued to make friends everywhere I went. I was only seven, and I did not really care about what people thought of me, except for this one time. Some neighborhood boys ditched me and I did not understand why. I felt abandoned. My mom was furious and told the boys' parents what their children had done. Then she told me they were not worth my energy if they were going to act like that. She was right, just as you know what and whom you need to eliminate from your life to align with who you are and to keep your vibration high for a joyful and abundant life.

Some of the choices we have to make while we are on Earth appear painful. Maybe we don't know how to get out of the situation, or maybe we have fear around it. Many of you feel there are no other options. There are always choices and options. Stop using this as an excuse.

It made me feel so good when my mom stuck up for me with those boys. I knew someone had my back. In life, we don't always feel like someone has our back. Sometimes we can feel alone and no one understands what we've been through, what we're going through, and how hopeless all of this makes us feel. You are never alone. You always have a connection to your Soul Self, all of your helpers, and your loved ones. I talk a lot about the Soul Self in this book because this is the connection that is the most important. You can connect with your loved ones, angels, guides, and whoever else, but the strongest connection you can have is with your Soul Self.

Much of what your loved ones and I do now is assist people trying to find their way. We work hard at connecting with those who need help, and bring peace and hope to them. You do not have to wait for us to come, however. You can call on us and ask for advice about the decisions you need to make. You do not need to call a particular helper to come help you. You can simply ask for assistance from those of us in high vibration for your highest good. You will be amazed at how the doors open and choices appear. We were there all along but maybe you couldn't see us. It takes teamwork to fulfill a lifetime of lessons and this is what we in Heaven do for you—provide what you need to successfully maneuver through the life you requested.

We cannot intervene unless you ask for our help because of free will. I talked about this in another chapter, but I emphasize this again because asking for our help is simple. You say, "Please help me with this situation, those of high vibration, so I can see all of my options. Please help me get where I need to go for my highest good."

As humans, people make things complicated. In order to receive Divine help, they expect to pay a price ahead of time or follow certain rituals to get what they need. This is not true. As you are discovering in reading this book, it is much more about intention, meaning you say what you want to have happen instead of complaining about what you don't want to have happen and allowing abundance to be brought to you. Your loved ones and helpers, and even your Soul Self cannot fix your life because this is up to you. Once you figure out the formula, it is a smooth path. As a part of your lesson, obstacles are placed in front of you because you need to learn to move out of the way and allow life to flow.

Going back to the beginning of the chapter when I said how you need to be observant of what you bring into your energy field, this is true about those from whom you seek advice on the physical plane and those you have around you on a daily basis. It is not only the news you need to turn off, but also any negative speak about yourself, your life, your obstacles, your idiosyncrasies and any other part of your life where you might be too critical of yourself. Those in your life who are critical of you and tell you their disempowering opinions need to be warned that negativity is not part of your reality anymore and they have the choice to stop talking to you like that or not be a part of your life. It sounds harsh and many of these people will be very dramatic about your response to them, but you know who these people are and whether they support you or drain you.

How many times have you seen a post on Facebook that says something to the effect of "I'm tired of all of you criticizing me so I'm going to unfriend you all so you can't do this to me anymore"? What that person is trying to say is "I'm tired of people telling me I'm not worth a darn and I'm not gonna take it anymore." And why should they? Why should anyone accept from another human being that they are less than, unworthy, insignificant, ugly, or stupid? This is not why you are on the planet. For some of you it is a lesson in personal power.

Again, I say turn off the news, remove anything draining your energy from your life, even if it is a person or people, and say yes to having an abundant life where you have personal power and are living for your highest good. This is what your Soul Self wants for you. This is also what your loved ones in Heaven want for you, no matter who they were on Earth and what lessons they brought you. Your loved ones have a very different perspective now. They see their part in your life experience and understand what you need and want to do while you are on Earth. For some it's crazy to think your loved one would care at all based upon their actions while on the planet. They were in their human suit, which made such a difference in how they responded to you and your experiences with them. Things have changed now. They know who you are, your Soul Self, and they delight in every advancement you make on your path. It is okay to ask for their support. Or not. They are not hurt when you don't talk to them or feel like you need to consult with a higher source instead of them. At the same time, they are happy to watch you and smile at all of your successes. They are on your team. It does not matter who you ask to help you. We will be there with bells on!

CHAPTER TEN
Layers Upon Layers

W e have covered quite a few different ideas and concepts so far. The next part of this book is about the multidimensional aspects of you and of us in Heaven. We are all multidimensional because we are in bodies and in spirit at the same time. I would like to update the definition of multidimensional to those souls who are in more than two dimensions, or states of energy, at the same time. My mom, for example, is a multidimensional soul because she has her earthly awareness in many dimensions and parts of her Soul Self in many dimensions. Many of you have chosen to do this now to make the best use of your energy, and propel the planet forward so we can get where we need to go.

Where do we need to go? We need to get Earth out of the dimension she is in. Truthfully, she is already in higher dimensions but there is a lag because of heavy energy on the planet. As I stated before, many of us are helping her energy so she can move into the higher dimensions. Along with this, we want all souls on Earth to be in the higher dimensions. This will take some radical shifting, as you can imagine. If you look at the events on the planet now, it is clear there is shifting taking place and this will continue until the job is done. I want to go back to the concept that everything we do on the planet has a plan, a design, or lesson of some sort. The events on Earth, such as mass killings or destruction through natural disasters are not random at all. These are planned events to assist the souls who want to leave the planet and fulfill their contract in other ways. These other ways could be helping their loved ones to understand they are all right and to let go of anger about the unfairness of the event, whatever that might have been. When there is a mass exodus of energy from the planet, the souls who leave help us hold the energy for all of you. From your perspective it is hard to see these events as being planned, so I want to remind you nothing happens to anything or to anyone who has not agreed in advance to have it occur. There are no exceptions to this. The sooner you accept this, the faster you can get your job done in your Universe.

There are many on your planet who have come from other dimensions. They may have human form or not. They have come to help so there's no reason for fear. Those from other planets or dimensions that are not helping but try to hinder our progress are being removed from Earth's energy. You don't need to worry about this any longer. We do not want you to invest any energy in it. Invest energy into helpers who have come from other places, very faraway places, who require our assistance to get the job done. These might be your neighbors, teachers, the person at the grocery store, anyone you encounter. The objective of the entire Universe is to move Earth into the higher dimensions along with all of its inhabitants. Your loved ones are helping also because we are all part of the same system. We are connected to everyone and everything so it is in your loved ones' best interest and yours to have success in this area.

By now you are asking, "How can this be? There is so much despair, cruelty, and unfairness on the planet." We see this too and are doing everything we can to change this.

High vibration and frequency are all around you. You just need to tap in to it and stay in that space. It is easier than you believe. Those on your planet who stay in this high frequency space can deal with stress and the demands of the planet because they know there is purpose to everything happening and do not get caught up in the drama or emotional charge. This can be said also for your loved ones who have passed. They understand what needs to happen and that everything revolves around energy.

Going back to the multidimensional concept, those who are on your planet from multiple dimensions and have their energy in Earth's and other frequencies can be thought of as straddling different worlds. Their Soul Self might originate within our system or, as I talked about earlier, many other systems and places in our Universe. My mom and I are from a small star system near Pleiades. We know of other souls working with my mom who are from the Sirius area, and those are just two of the millions of places from which souls have traveled to incarnate on Earth. The Earth and Solar System is very new in relation to other parts of the Universe. It is a playground for many souls who want to explore other ways of existing.

If you were to try to comprehend the different levels of energy that have come to the planet to assist, it might look like the layers of energy. It is more about frequency than about layers, but let's use the layer example so I can better explain this idea. The layer on which your body resides is called the third layer. The other two layers did not work very well, and we do not access them anymore. The fourth layer is an area of frequency very close to Earth's frequency and many reside there because they enjoy being close to Earth energy but they may not wish to have a body to restrict them. The fifth layer is where your loved ones go when they leave their bodies. They do need to pass through the fourth layer but it usually is not a place where many stay because it's still dense like Earth. In the fifth layer, the energy and frequency is much higher and we can accomplish things using only thoughts. Our energy does not need to be replenished as often as when we are in the fourth layer. Many of your loved ones stay in this fifth layer for some time as they make sure you are all right and direct you through thoughts and messages. Most souls then move to the sixth layer. The frequency there is much higher. There is a Universal sound that is heard continuously when you are in the sixth layer. It is like a tone or note that plays repeatedly. This is created by the frequency of the souls here. Many souls then move to the seventh layer which we call the layer of creation. This is not to imply you cannot create in the other layers, but in the seventh layer creation is instantaneous and does not require substance. When you create in the seventh layer, you are building from thought and it immediately becomes a creation. Many of the remedies for illness and scientific breakthroughs come from the seventh layer.

When a soul moves to the eighth layer, its energy becomes more intertwined with other energies in that layer, and they create a collective energy for specific purposes. These purposes could be for more creation on different planets or creation of thoughts, new materials, and can be a planning environment for other planets and life forms. Those in the ninth layer work on structures, biological configurations such as life forms. The ninth layer has many energies who are called upon to heal on Earth because they understand biological structures intimately. The tenth layer is focused on thoughts and mind creation. An energy from the tenth layer would not understand anything about emotional attachment. If you remember Spock from the series *Star Trek*[5], he is a good representation of those in the tenth layer. The eleventh layer has incredibly high frequency and tones to the point that they emit this incredibly bright golden light. They sparkle intensely. They are pure energy and their purpose is to create physical worlds of light for souls to visit to receive cleansing and renewal so they may go back in to whatever system they desire and experience more from different frequencies. Imagine a gleaming car wash as the soul rejuvenates within the layers of light and comes out squeaky clean, ready for the next adventure. The twelfth layer in our system is one of the highest layers and it is where the core of energies resides and watches over all souls and energies within our system. You can think of this as the executive branch of the government, but without the hierarchy. There is no hierarchy where I am.

This is how our system works. There are many other layers in other systems because the energy within our Universe is infinite. I wanted to break down the layers up to the twelfth so you can understand how it works.

I have tried to keep it as simple as possible. Because of the way the human brain works, it is hard to comprehend the entirety of what I am experiencing in Heaven, but you need to know how incredibly powerful our system is. It is not chaotic at all. There is a flow of energy, and within that flow is the ultimate plan for your life.

I told you earlier my mother and I are from Pleiades and we came here with countless other energies to begin the project of planet Earth. We are certainly not alone in this endeavor. It takes planning and changes in the designs to create a place where souls can incarnate into bodies to experience a particular life form unlike any other in the Universe. Many of us have been incarnating on planet Earth for many years. We try different things and ways to experience life and will continue to do so. Each time we have a lifetime and come back home, we share what we have learned with the Creator. It is a unified energy at the core of our system that has asked us to assist the collective by experiencing all facets of incarnation. The Creator creates more energy based upon what we have learned and shared. The Creator, again, is not one energy, but a collective energy. If you remember earlier, I talked about the collective energies in the higher layers. The Creator takes parts of its creations and brings them back into itself to help expand its energy and understand more. Each time the Creator energy receives more information it becomes bigger. We are always eager to return home so we can share what we have learned with the Creator because when the Creator energy expands, we expand as well. We have so much fun telling our Creator about all of our adventures and what we learned.

Before we convey information to the Creator, we have a life review. During this review, we look at all of the aspects of our life from that body. With the help of one of our council members reviewing the life with us, we are able to see things from others' perspectives and from the higher perspective. What we do not see are the excuses about why we did certain things or responded in certain ways because this no longer matters. This is a critical part of coming home because we cannot tell our Creator what we learned if we don't see it for ourselves. It's like a big movie screen and we get to watch a rerun of the lifetime. We stop on certain scenes and discuss what happened with the council member. Having a second pair of eyes as we are reviewing and learning is helpful because even though we are not in a body anymore, we might not see what we are supposed to see from the experience. We pause every now and then to take notes on what was expected from the scene and what actually happened. Then we make a list of the things we did and did not learn. Most of this is done through thought, and it's not like we actually have to write it down. The state of energy in which we are at that moment is capable of retaining all of this information. We are not limited to the human brain anymore.

It is very exciting when we look over the lifetime and see what we accomplished in that body. Some of you might think it is scary to see the things that were not done as well as you wanted, but, from our perspective, it is about learning and moving forward. We have no regrets, no guilt about what we did or didn't do, and we understand the effects of our thoughts and actions in every one of the situations we review. For many, the list of items, concepts, or feelings we did not get when we were in that body is the prescription for the next incarnation.

I want to make it clear that we choose when we come back into bodies. We are not forced to come back because we didn't do things right in a lifetime. We are given options by our council when things are put together for possible incarnations. We are never coerced into going back into a body to experience a life. It is about understanding who we are and what we need to do to get to the highest level possible so we can show the Creator what it's like on Earth. I talked about this a little bit before, but it's vital to understand the concept: it is not an eye for an eye. When we choose to go back into a body to experience life from another person's perspective, maybe that of someone we hurt or did not get along with, we are doing it because we want to learn what it is like for the other person. It is never because we were bad in a lifetime, like we did terrible things to people or to ourselves.

The justice system on your planet is not carried into Heaven. We do not require such a structure because once you come home, you understand how your actions affected those involved and there is an immediate recognition that the energy must be balanced. How we balance that energy is up to us. A lot of this can be done from where we are in Heaven, but many choose to have another experience on Earth to take the lesson to a much deeper level. The same can be said for your loved ones and their response to any emotional issues you may have in your current life. They love you very much, but because they do not have the same requirement for engaging emotionally, they do not see the situation as you may see it. What they see is your request for the lesson or your choice to move down a path. How you move down the path is inconsequential to them as long as you have the desired result, meaning the lesson is learned. I talk about this because one day you will walk into a medium's office and the advice your loved one gives you might sound a little different than when they were in a body. It is because they are no longer limited to the emotional attachments and barriers of being in a body. They see things from the higher perspective and respond accordingly.

Let's say you are married. Your mother was Catholic, and to her death was adamant against divorce because her religion forbade it. You want to get a divorce, and you are concerned your mother, now in Heaven, would tell you under no circumstances should you leave this person, regardless of what he or she had done to you. You walk into the medium's office and ask to speak to your mother to get her permission for divorce. Expecting the worst, you brace yourself because you feel she will tell you, or guilt you, into staying in the marriage. You are surprised when she says it is for your highest good to be on your own. This is what I mean when I say your loved ones in Heaven understand things from a detached perspective. Your mother is not attached to her religion anymore and agrees leaving the marriage is for your highest good so you can find your personal power, who you are, and what you came to do.

It's quite possible your mother had her life review and saw what religion did as far as holding her back and creating limits, not only for her but her family. She sees now we have no limits and her beliefs did not support who she was as a soul. Honestly, no religion can support who you are because they are based upon a "one size fits all" model, whereas we are all individuals and have different needs and desires. In Heaven, we understand why people would continue to stay within organized religion because it offers answers to questions about Heaven and Earth and what happens when we die. Most of us want to believe there is something greater than us and we find the closest representation to this in a religion so we can feel as if we have more of an idea of the mysteries of life and death. There is nothing wrong with this option unless you infringe upon someone else's desires to seek their own truth about their life and their views on life after death.

Getting back to the life review, once we have seen our life from a different perspective and have the input from our council member, we lay out our next step. Many of us choose to wait until our soul family members come home before we move into a new set of incarnations because we like having the relationships with our soul family, especially since we move through lives together to learn lessons of similar nature. We have more fun deciding who is going to have what role and laugh at the possibilities as we contemplate being back in bodies. The concepts I discussed in earlier chapters about the amount of energy we bring into our bodies are critical in understanding this. We definitely can hop back into another lifetime even when our loved ones are still incarnated because we have plenty of energy to do this. We only take a percentage of our Soul Self energy into each life. We can have multiple lives on Earth and elsewhere at the same time. There is no time or space in Heaven, so it doesn't matter when our soul family returns.

We can also choose to stay in Heaven and learn from here for a while. The jobs are endless, really. We have nurses, doctors, scientists, teachers, and creators, to name a few. I am doing quite a few things at once. I love to create, as I have said before. I create on a very large scale, such as planets, and on a very small scale, such as plants and other life forms. I am gathering energies to help Earth, and I am holding Earth's energy. I am also helping my mom with her students and clients so they can connect with their loved ones in Heaven. My specialty is communication, so I am often requested to assist on different projects requiring this expertise.

Your loved one might have been a successful electrician in his life on Earth, so he might choose to work with different forms of electricity here. It is at a much higher level than the circuits on Earth, but the concepts are similar.

The nurses and doctors use their knowledge to help those in their profession on Earth when their services are needed. This might be in the form of giving a doctor the correct diagnosis when he or she can't seem to figure out what is wrong with someone. It could be correcting the medication a nurse is about to give you as you lie in your hospital bed after a surgery or illness. These professions in Heaven are the helping professions. They help those on Earth with the living.

Teachers and scholars are abundant in certain layers of Heaven. They teach those who wish to stay at these layers in settings similar to colleges or places of higher learning on Earth. As I said in the earlier chapters, we love to learn here. Some choose to stay in the layers closer to Earth so they can study in these "schools." This would especially be true if the soul was planning to head back into another body.

Our specialty in Heaven may not have anything to do with what we did on Earth. Sometimes we choose a life that has nothing to do with what we know. These are exciting lives because we get to learn something new about ourselves and expand. If you can imagine a child who just learned to ride a bike running to tell her mom about her adventure, this is how we feel when we have tried something new on Earth and then come back to tell our Creator about the experience. It is exhilarating, and we magnify our energy and that of our Universe even further.

CHAPTER ELEVEN
The Way We Die

I t is very important we talk about different passings because there are huge misconceptions on Earth about them and how these affect our travels to Heaven.

Let's discuss suicide first. Suicide is the taking of one's own life, creating certain situations for the family left behind. I want to remind you that there is no judgment where I am, so when this happens, these souls are not judged by anyone in Heaven.

There are many reasons why souls end their lives. It could be they were supposed to leave at a different date and missed that opportunity, or they have a difficult time adjusting to Earth and its denseness. It might be they were ambitious with the lessons they wanted to learn and couldn't quite learn them. Regardless, we do not see suicide as a mistake. We understand the ramifications for those left behind on the planet and we address the issue accordingly. Remember when I said nothing happens unless it is supposed to happen? This is true regardless of how the person leaves. Let's say someone takes his life and his little brother finds him. This incident, the brother finding the body, would have occurred regardless of how the person exited. This does not mean it hurts less or that scarring will not occur, but it does mean there are complications the person who took his life needs to remedy. When souls leave in this manner, they have the same opportunities as anyone else to raise their tone and vibration and get to the higher levels of energy. Some do not do this immediately because they feel they are unworthy due to the dogma practiced on

Earth around this way of passing, or because they are very concerned about the wellbeing of their family since they can see how their suicide affected them.

Those who took their lives do have a life review in Heaven after they raise their tone and get to a higher level of energy. It is in this place where they can re-experience their time on Earth, including their passing, from other people's perspectives. This can be a scary proposition if these souls feel they did an egregious act, so they may choose to stay at the previous level of the energy for some time. We do our best in Heaven to demonstrate how much we love them regardless of their actions and send helpers if they need it. It is okay if they choose to not move quickly up the levels of energy. We understand the difficulties in releasing some of the Earthly perceptions in order to see the bigger picture. Our ultimate goal is to show them they are capable of balancing the energy with those they affected with their choice of passing. After a life review, they can balance the energy from here as a soul or go back into another body to work it out a different way. Many choose to stay here for a time and assist others on Earth who might be contemplating a similar exit. They impress upon the living the ramifications from departing in that manner—that it might not be worth the relief of taking such an exit in that lifetime.

These souls also have the opportunity to renew themselves and isolate their energy so all denser energies from their passing are removed. This is similar to the energy cleansing I described in earlier chapters where the energy is "scrubbed" clean and restored for that soul.

You might ask, "Are suicides ever contracted?" and the answer is yes. In these cases, all those involved have agreed to it and are eager to learn what their souls need to learn from surviving the loss of a loved one to suicide. Are these the norm? It is an interesting question because there is so much happening on the planet and it would appear more people are leaving by taking their own lives than at any other time. Many of these cases are contracts and others are not. Because we have numerous energies from other places in the Universe who want this human experience, sometimes these souls are aggressive in the lessons they want to learn. Since they are not used to the denseness of the planet, they have a harder time adjusting and may choose to leave earlier than their plan intended. We do not see these as failings. Everyone acquires some knowledge in the situation, and all are grateful for the opportunity for advanced learning. From your Earthly perspective, these ideas may sound preposterous. After all, who in their right mind would agree to have a loved one, especially a child, leave by suicide? These are the special souls who take learning very seriously and strive for advancement in their energy to a very high degree. These are not newbies. The ones who are leaving by suicide quite possibly are from elsewhere in the Universe. Also, the ones affected by these decisions, those still in bodies, are certainly not new to the planet.

I am talking about this extensively because your planet has huge hang-ups about suicide, and these perceptions need to be changed. If you have a loved one who took his or her life, rest assured they are being cared for and learning in amazing ways.

Another way of leaving I want to discuss is accidental overdose. Not only does this affect younger kids, but it also affects older adults. These overdoses can be the result of prescription or recreational drugs. When we talk about prescription drugs, there's a tendency to blame the pharmacist or doctor who prescribed the drugs, but honestly, this is such a peaceful way to go. I am surprised more people don't choose this manner of exit. When we talk about children overdosing, of course there are other things to consider such as the child's use of illegal drugs, the obtaining of such drugs, and why a child would do such a thing. Parents blame themselves and those around the child. After all, shouldn't we have seen the signs, shouldn't we have done something to help the child? It is critical to understand that if a child leaves by overdose, it is the choice of the higher self. In these cases, there are always lessons for the parents, teachers, friends, and anyone else who is affected. Sometimes those lessons are about self-forgiveness. Sometimes they are about letting go of the guilt. Maybe it is a wakeup call to change behavior. I can say one hundred percent of the time it is not about the child who leaves but rather about those who are left on Earth. There is always a lesson, but it does not mean you did something wrong. One huge lesson, regardless of the person's age, is to not blame others for what happened. There is no blame because, if you recall, that person chose to exit in that manner. It is no one's fault, even when it is a medical mistake. Your challenge, if you have a loved one who left in this manner, is to let it go. It does not matter how you do this or how long it takes, it will assist you beyond words if you are able to let it go.

Cancer is another subject I wish to discuss. Cancer was created because souls wanted to experience the disintegration of the body. Those who leave by cancer have agreed to this as well, and this includes children. Those children with childhood cancers are the bravest of the brave, as anyone who attended these children as their bodies cease to function can attest. Only the strongest of souls attempt this exit as children.

Adults with cancer are a little different. This disease has many functions. It can identify the weak energy areas in your body in order to give you the opportunity to correct what you are doing to your body and continue to live a functional life. The body is an incredibly complicated organism and there are many factors that account for the contracting of cancer cells. These include dietary, emotional, energetic, and mental aspects. There are basic questions for anyone who has been diagnosed with cancer. "Was I eating what I was supposed to eat?" "Was I supporting my body emotionally?" "Did I come in with any energetic blocks or were any blocks created in my life?" "What is my mental perception of why I got cancer?" I don't necessarily want to go into every detail about this disease because there are many facets and each case is different. For many, a cancer diagnosis is a wakeup call to change something in their energetic makeup and being, including removing blocks, eating right, believing in the power of healing and self-love. For others, this is the exit choice they made prior to coming into their body. Regardless of what they do to remedy the current situation, they have chosen to leave from the disease.

Whenever there is a long convalescence, especially one which appears painful to the body, our loved ones on Earth worry about our transition to Heaven. There are some circumstances where transition might take longer than others, but for the most part, near the end of that lifetime, there are plenty of visitations from loved ones in Heaven to assure the person all is well and it's okay to let go of the physical. Usually at that point, the soul knows what to do and rises out of the body, relieved and pain free.

Many souls incarnated now have chosen to leave by way of mental instability or dysfunction. Dementia, Alzheimer's and other mental disorders are more common than even ten years ago. Again, the soul chooses this malady as a means of learning and exploring what it is like to not be able to rely on mental functions. What happens when the body finally succumbs to the disease? Those with these mental dysfunctions also have extensive help in transitioning from body to energy. These souls usually take a little more time to adjust back to their energetic state only because we do take some of our mind functions with us and these functions need to be restored for these individuals prior to their life review. This can be done in many ways including the energy cleansing I spoke about earlier in this chapter, as well as isolation and renewing. These souls can still be reached through a medium during their time of renewal, but the connection might be a little fuzzy. Experienced mediums will know how to strengthen the connection, so please don't ever think you cannot contact loved ones who left under these conditions.

There are more and more younger kids on the planet who are diagnosed with mental instability, diseases, and dysfunctions. Many of these are by choice. These souls want to see if they can "fix" themselves without having to medicate. If you are the parent of one of these souls, you have also chosen to be a part of your child's life. It is critical for you to stop blaming and wondering why you are being punished in this manner because it is not about that at all. It is about you learning to be an unlimited soul, understanding you have a heart connection with your child regardless of their capacities or incapacities, and your soul is advancing quickly by agreeing to these circumstances. The way you can help these children is to see them as the souls they are and listen to them with your heart.

There is a misperception about drowning I wish to clarify. This also is a peaceful way to exit. It may not look like this from the surface, but I can assure you if your loved one left by drowning, they had no trouble coming out of their body and transitioning to spirit. Many old souls choose to leave in this manner because it is a very easy passing. Many of these souls have assistance prior to the incident so they know exactly what to do when everything is happening. This might not be on a conscious level but occurs nonetheless.

If your loved ones were by themselves when they passed, please know they were not alone or afraid. You can't even imagine the assistance they have in these cases and, for that matter, all cases. We would not allow the soul to be alone unless he or she said it was the preferred way to exit.

If your loved one left before you were able to arrive to say goodbye, it was not because he or she did not love you but rather you were not supposed to be there when he or she passed. It is as simple as that. There does not have to be a reason for this although most of the time there is. It could be you were not supposed to see the person in their current state, or it was to challenge you to not fall into regret and guilt. Your loved ones in Heaven never want you to be in regret or guilt because those are wasted emotions and energy. Regret and guilt serve no purpose other than to make you feel less than, which does not serve your highest good. Please remember this if you are in the situation where you are not able to say goodbye or could not fulfill your loved ones' wishes. Honestly, they don't mind. They love you unconditionally and want only the best for you and their soul family.

You may be wondering what you chose for your exit. This information might be a bit more than you can handle being in a body, so we would say it's probably best if you continue to live and learn with what resonates with your soul. On the other hand, reading this section might be a wakeup call for you. We encourage you to evaluate your life circumstances right now. Does the path you are on serve you? Is it for your highest good? You have free will to change your life for the better.

Do not accept what people tell you just because they tell it to you and you consider them to be an authority. Always run everything you hear and read through your intuition meter. You know what is best for you. Trust you are given all the information you need to make the appropriate choice for any situation in your life. Remove the fear around how you exit the world and embrace the way you live. Souls line up to experience our planet, with its apparent hardship, harshness, and tragedy. If you are familiar with William Shakespeare, you may remember: "All the world's a stage, and all the men and women merely players; they have their exits and their entrances, and one man in his time plays many parts.[6]"

Shakespeare understood what we are doing on Earth. He knew our world is just a big set for the most incredible performances imaginable. There is a beautiful Oscar waiting for each of you when you finish your play and come home, including a standing ovation from your adoring fans.

CHAPTER TWELVE
Choosing How We Live

How do we select our new lives on Earth? Some of you who are incarnated now will want to come back and experience something different, and others will decide to not come back and stay in another state of energy. For those who decide they did not complete their lessons, they will get to choose from varying scenarios, what works best for them, and where they feel they can excel best. We get the opportunity to choose the basics of our lives—who is going to play mom, dad, brother, sister, etc. We often like to have the same players when we come into lives because of the familiarity and because our soul family knows how to get the job done. Consider this: everyone you meet is someone you have chosen to meet at that moment and they have agreed to play a part in your play. There are no exceptions to this. Sometimes the play gets changed in the middle of Act 1, Scene 20, but this only means there might be new players coming on the scene who have an expertise in the lesson you want to learn or in the job you hope to accomplish. We can create new scenes at anytime. There have been many points in your life where the scene was changed because it wasn't working or flowing the way it needed to. Everything is intertwined, though, and all of it has purpose.

When we get ready to choose a life, we ask for all of the players to agree to the basics of what we want to accomplish and discuss what they want to accomplish so they can also learn their lessons. Not everything is figured out, of course, because that would be boring. There is excitement in preparing to be in a body with a basic plan—not everything is known or a given. The way we interact in bodies is quite different than outside of our bodies. As we arrange the scenarios, we forget much of the complications we have on Earth. We look at it as an experience and satisfying our need for growth and expansion.

We get the basics of who we are, who the other players are and when they enter into our lives. Then we pick times for our entries into our bodies. For me, I chose to come four weeks prior to when I was actually due. My lungs were not fully developed which made it easier for me to leave later when I caught the flu in March 2007. It was not the flu that made my body stop working; it was the scar tissue in my lungs from my birth which made it harder for my immune system to fight the virus. I chose this way to leave. I knew this prior to coming into my life as J.T.

There are so many intricacies of our lifetimes, and it is difficult to explain in words. Our lives are like webs that stretch out expansively. Each time we make a decision, we move along a portion of our web, taking turns going backwards, moving forwards. The most important thing to remember is that we always end up where we need to be, even if we veer off course for years and years. It is about the journey and not the destination. This is what makes it so fascinating to souls in the Universe who partake in this game. We get to experience it however we want, and our supporting cast is eager to accommodate our wishes and help us learn, even if it means appearing as if they don't have the highest intentions. At the same time we are helping our soul family members in learning and experiencing what they want from their lifetimes.

Should we take an "unplanned" turn, all is well. We will learn from the detour as free will suggests, and eventually come back to the place in our web where we are experiencing what we asked to experience. There are no mistakes or failures. Sometimes we give our helpers in Heaven a run for their money because we make big changes in our plan as we fly along in our lives, and it is up to our Heavenly guides to accommodate the detours and assist in moving us back into the area from which we can accomplish our goals. Our helpers don't jump in right away because it is possible we will figure it out on our own. Should it look as if we are not able to move back into the learning space we requested, events will occur to nudge us toward this.

Before we come into bodies we are given options of how we want the scenario to appear. Imagine creating an entire play or script around your desires and wants. How exciting is that! We have countless options from which to choose since there are many ways we can learn. Our Life Planning Advisors, some call them the Council, present options in movie format so we can see what it might be like to live through that scenario. The Advisors give opinions on what might work best, but ultimately the choice is ours. We can choose to stay in spirit form longer or take a body. This is important because many believe the definition of karma is a forcing into another lifetime to right the wrongs we did to others. This is not the case. It never was and never will be. We are willing recipients and players because we see what is best for everyone involved and aim to convert energy into a higher form, one that balances the energy between souls.

We always strive to balance energy as quickly as possible because we understand the implications of having an energy system out of balance on Earth. It creates complications for many individuals, as you can attest from your current experiences on the planet. We can say with certainty that the energy on Earth is not balanced at the present time. That is not to say individuals are not working their hardest to balance the energy for themselves and others, but it does mean we have more to do to get planet Earth where she needs to be. Our aspirations when we choose a body are to assist not only our energy but everyone's. Remember, we are all connected, so what I do affects you and what you do affects me. If we all work at creating balance, then we can also assist those who are unaware of how their energy affects the rest of us.

One of the things we agree to do when we come in to balance the energy is to be kind to every living thing. The other is to remember how connected we are to everything. We seem to forget this when we make it into a body. Even the highest souls who enter into bodies have this experience. It's part of the journey. Our job is to learn or re-learn our connection so that we can accomplish much more than if we are unaware. You may notice many of the souls entering bodies these days do remember their connection but are often chastised or forced into the mold that has been created over the years. "Conform or else!" These individuals are highly evolved souls and have agreed to step into the denseness of Earth to help us remember and remove the space between the worlds. They have quite a job ahead of them because humans are creatures of habit and don't like it when something new comes into their world. They feel threatened and react by trying to force these souls into doing things the old way. This will not work because this is not what these souls came to do. They came to show us how our structures are weak and we need to rebuild based upon the understanding that we all are connected on our planet and everywhere else. Instead of listening to them, many unknowing parents choose to medicate their children. We want you to know this is not the course of action for these children. You must change, not them. Stop medicating and start listening to these souls. They have much to teach and they understand much more about their purpose in the short time on the planet than most adults do in their entire lifetimes.

This is also true for the education of these individuals. They require a different kind of learning, so putting them in standard classroom situations is not effective. I tell you this because each of you have met one of these beautiful souls who agreed to come change the planet with us, and you know in your heart that what worked for the children in the past no longer works for the children of today. We want you to take special notice of these individuals and assist them in whatever way you feel is in line with your purpose and lessons. Again, if you are reading this book, you have said you want to learn more about who you are and your place in the Universe. This is one way to help all souls. How you manifest this is up to you because it is different for everyone. Some are called to teach these children while others are called to support them. Others are called to walk beside them and let them know they are not crazy; they were just born into a crazy world.

Once we have made the decision to enter into a body, the play begins. The way the human body is constructed, you are given time in your mother's womb to adjust to your body. During this time, you may come in and out of that body at will. You do not have to stay in it until the moment of your birth, but most choose to stay in their bodies for the last couple of months to really get acclimated to their new costume. During this time in the womb, we experience life from a protected point of view, unless we asked to have a different experience, such as toxic substances coming into our bodies or deformities that would support the lessons we wanted to learn. Yes, anyone who is born with any deformities or anomalies has asked for this to occur. We are not helpless babies, by any means. We are souls who are excited to experience the world in different ways and from diverse perspectives. I cannot stress this enough. Whatever happens to us, no matter what age, is in our life plan. That does not mean you should turn your back on helpless babies, but please put it into perspective when you hear on the news about something that happens to a baby. I go back to our contracts to explain this. If a baby is hurt in any way, all parties have agreed to this result.

While we are in the womb, we have plenty of time to go over our plan with our guides, helpers, and those assisting us in bodies. As you recall, we still hold much of our energy in Heaven, so we can all regroup if one of us wants to alter things and create new scenarios even if we are already in bodies.

We also have plenty of help to acclimate to our new surroundings. For me, the energy named Hope who assisted me out of my body when I left in March 2007 also helped me go into my body by being with me in the womb. Just as when we leave our bodies we are never alone, we are not alone when we enter our bodies either. Hope and I are of the same soul energy. We agreed to help each other in this lifetime. There is a constant connection to our family in Heaven, and the support and love from the entire Universe is accessible anytime.

You may ask why we agree to forget everything. Wouldn't it be easier if we remembered who we are and what we are supposed to do so we could get it done? I hope by now you understand the answer to this question. It is because we want to learn our own way. Again, the whole purpose of this is to grow and expand who we are as souls, and this would not be done effectively if we knew the plan. The point is to *not* know the plan and follow-through anyway. It would be boring if we knew what we were supposed to learn and how. This concept will not change even in the New Earth when we have successfully and permanently brought Earth's frequency to a higher level. What will change is the access we have to information in the higher realms.

Life can be easy, and life can be hard. The choice is yours and depends on your observations of your life and how you choose to adjust to these observations.

If you have not heard about the New Earth, let me describe it to you. There are many definitions of the New Earth from philosophers, channelers, and others who are supporting the changes in Earth's energy at this time. The New Earth is a place we hope to create where there is not as much pain and suffering but still a place to learn lessons and to grow and expand as an energy and soul. The energy on planet Earth has become so dense, it is harder for her to support everyone, as we discussed in earlier chapters. Changes are needed to lighten the energy of all inhabitants. The point is to remove lower vibrations, energies not supporting other souls on the planet, and replace them with higher energies and souls who want to learn in differently. We are so stuck in what we think life should be that we forgot the whole point of this play. Part of this has to do with the incredible aggressiveness some of you have in learning your lessons and how you believe you can overcome previous obstacles. Sometimes the denseness is just too much and it takes over the plan, which doesn't work for anybody. Our goal is to have as much high vibration energy on the planet as we can, lifting Earth to the higher levels and layers we discussed in earlier chapters. In order to this, the energy needs to change.

First and foremost, those who interfere with others' plans need to be removed and may not return to Earth. For this to happen, the majority of the souls on Earth need to agree they have the power to make changes in their lives. They can say and manifest what is for their highest good, which is to remove these energies. We can't take these dense energies off the planet because of free will, although the earlier civilizations such as Atlantis and Lemuria as well as the Mayans were all removed at once by the request of the many souls being affected. With Atlantis and Lemuria, power had run amok and souls who had connection to the higher realms were not using it for everyone's highest good. We decided it was time to start over and removed all of the souls except for a few. With the Mayans, they were not harming others but were going to be harmed by some other civilizations on the planet at the time. It was not their plan to be harmed, so we removed them from Earth and brought them back home.

We don't want to do this again. We want to continue the learning we have begun and have a place for all souls to expand their energy in such a way as to help all of us expand. To do this, things need to change. We cannot allow the denser energies to control us and others. We must find the light within each of us, remember how connected we are, and remember what we're here to do. In doing this, we open ourselves to the amazement of all the planet has to offer and to all of the support from the helpers in Heaven. We do not want Earth to become a dark planet. We have worked hard to get to where we are, and that includes everyone reading this book. We are very excited about the advancements in energy and the raising of the frequency of Earth and her occupants. It is quite a vast production which requires the assistance of everyone. We are grateful to all of you who want a better life for you and your fellow beings. The way you can help is to keep your tone and frequency at the highest level possible and not allow others to take your energy from you in any way. We all have a vested interest in creating a higher vibration planet. We will still be able to learn our lessons and expand our souls, but it will be in a very different format, which will be a great relief to so many of us, especially Mother Earth.

Remember, you are part of the whole and the whole is a part of you, and anything you do affects everything on the planet and beyond. The best thing you can do is to mind your own energy and keep it high. The higher, the better. As the energy of the whole gets higher and higher, it is easier to move all of us into the other dimensions.

We understand that sometimes it feels like you are dragging the rest of the planet with you as you reach for higher dimensions. You wonder when those around you are going to "get it" so they can start pulling their own weight. At the same time, you know you have to make a better life for you and those you affect with your energy. This is critical in your purpose on Earth. We are so pleased at how quickly everyone is learning and how the tone of the planet is rising at a phenomenal rate. We want to thank of all of you who have participated in this endeavor, whether or not you realize your importance in this mission.

We are all here to make a difference. Even if you only are able to affect those people in your immediate circle, you are still creating something amazing with your life. We don't want you to compare yourself to others because it defeats the purpose of your learning and expanding. Only be concerned about your own energy. There's nothing you can do about your fellow being's energy. Remember free will. Judgment and resentment only hold you down. It is clear these elements must no longer be a part of your existence if you want to get to where you said you wanted to go. We are all here to do this work. No matter how insignificant your life might appear, realize now in this moment there is no insignificance anywhere in the Universe. You are a bright soul and are on Earth to do much more than what you might recall. I'm hoping as you read this book you remember more about your mission and how you said you wanted to assist with the transition from heavy to light.

Only you can manage you. It is for your highest good to figure out what this means for you. I can tell you what it means for us. With your help, we accomplish our goal. It's okay if others don't follow because, as I said before, the higher you go, the higher the planet goes, and we will bring the energy of the whole into the higher realms regardless of participation by all souls. In other words, we do not need everyone to understand and move with the higher tones in order to shift into the higher dimensions. By your participation, you assist those who might not understand that they have a part in the grand scheme.

We are so grateful to have all of the assistance we have at this time. It is imperative we continue moving forward in a positive manner, which is where you come in. All of the information I have given you in this book has hopefully opened your awareness to the incredible opportunities that exist for you on Earth. It is only the beginning. There are many more chapters of your story, of the life you get to create. Don't ever underestimate the power of thought and your ability to change anything in your reality that does not serve you. We all have this gift, and we can use it to create a world full of fascination, beauty, creativity, and wholeness. You are not just doing this for yourself but for everyone in our Universe.

This incredible web we call life gives us many options to move forward and learn from different perspectives. We are given many opportunities to grow and expand. Your mission now is to be aware and observe how others in your life are bringing you these opportunities. Learn what you need to learn from your teachers, who incidentally might appear as adversaries, so you can move on to the next adventure you asked to experience. Stop blaming others for your circumstances and start creating your own reality by understanding your part in the play. Everything you do affects the rest of the Universe, and now is the time to reclaim the leading role. You are a superstar, and we are your supporting cast to help you shine. What will you change now, knowing what you know about the purpose of your life on Earth?

Choose wisely and act immediately. And remember, you are never alone.

CHAPTER THIRTEEN
The Purpose of Life

Let's talk about the bigger scale of things. You know you are much bigger than the body you inhabit right now, and we, your helpers in Heaven, are much bigger than you may have recognized before reading this book. There is a vast, infinite energy from which you can draw should you need more to do your work on the planet.

Let me tell you how this works. You have accepted you are a grand soul, a part of a much bigger soul in a different dimension than what you can physically sense. You have access to this energy at any moment, night or day. We want you to receive energy from this infinite source to help you through your lessons and learning as you progress through life. Those days when you wake up feeling drained of energy, you can simply intend for more to fill you so you are refreshed and able to accomplish more. This is one of the gifts we give to you for being on the planet.

By now, I hope you realize that you create all of your reality entirely through intention and thought. If you do not, I suggest you go back to earlier chapters where we discussed these concepts. What you think about is what you get. If you think about lacking money, resources, or love, then you get more of that lack. If you think about all of the wonderful blessings you have in your life and have gratitude even though some of them do not appear as abundance, the energy around you and supporting you will give you more abundance and blessings. If you need more energy to complete a task, intend for that energy to come to you in the form of light or energy waves, or whatever you might need to accept the energy. We always state like attracts like, so keep your tone and frequency high and the energy you receive will be the same or greater.

You can also ask for different players to come in to play different parts. Be careful with this because you might not get what you think you want to receive. If someone gives you a lesson and you are not getting it, the Universe will respond with someone else who might be more abrupt in the lesson you are learning. You can also request ease and grace in learning your lessons because we want all of humanity to understand who they are and get the inside scoop on what we're all doing in Heaven, and this includes changing things and easing up when requested. Provided you acknowledge the lesson you receive and ask for ease and grace, we will oblige per your intention and instruction. That is, as long as your higher self did not request the harshness you are receiving. Usually this is not the case. So ask for it to come to you differently with ease and grace. Again, it is very important you acknowledge what the lesson is first.

The example below is from my mom:

In 2009 I was receiving the lesson of being comfortable with who I am, even if that meant being out of the norm and considered "evil" in some circles. This lesson came in various forms and from quite a few people in my circle of friends and acquaintances. I was getting my feet wet as a medium, which was difficult for many people to accept because of their belief system. At the same time, I was having difficulties with a business partner and some other people who I considered very dear to me. The common theme was having a situation arise where their interpretation of the events was significantly different than mine, and, from their perspective, I was behaving a certain way. From my perspective, obviously, it was a very different scenario. Along the way I would ask, "Am I the one who is crazy here?" "No, it is not you," J.T. would respond. Regardless, I felt persecuted and criticized for things I didn't do. I saw a pattern emerge after some time and finally asked, "What is the lesson I'm supposed to learn here and how do I get this to stop?" The answer was given to me indirectly because, after all, I was supposed to figure it out on my own. This was priming me for a very public career where not everyone would agree with what I had to say and many might actually be threatened by what I do and what I represent.

Many areas of my life were touched by this lesson. Once I realized my goal was to not react, I did my best to say nothing when accusations came to my attention. I was grateful when that lesson ended, or so I thought. In Spring 2010, I received the lesson again from a different group. Seeing this was related to the lessons the prior year, I worked diligently to not react and understand I am not responsible for what other people say or think about me. I asked for ease and grace in the process, and I am still learning how to not have it affect me so much.

If I see this lesson coming now, I can recognize it for what it is and be more allowing so the intended results are achieved. Such was the case in December 2012 when I was involved in an auto accident in a parking lot. I had no idea at the time I was going to be asked to experience the feelings of persecution again. In this incident, the witness to the accident had a very different version of the events than I. I was going to fight for my "innocence" until I realized it was the same old lesson. Once again, I had to let go of what other people said I did, even though it was not part of my truth.

As you see, sometimes the lessons for which we ask are in conflict with what we perceive as our morals and values. When my mom was being attacked from different groups of people, of course she was felt hurt and betrayed. She also knew what she had to do to get through it because she asked us for assistance.

Did she get to skip the lesson? No. She is on the planet just like everybody else. She has asked to learn her lessons and advance her soul just like you. Having communication with us does not give you a "get out of jail free" card. It does give insight and help to figure out these crazy things that happen in your lifetime.

We can help you, but you need to ask for the help. We need to know you understand that this is a lesson you asked to learn. Many of the prayers you send to us are prayers of desperation. The Universe responds to desperation with more of the same. This doesn't mean you stop praying because prayer is an intensely powerful intention. It means you can be even more directed with your prayer to get the desired results by changing the emotion around your prayer or request.

What is the difference between these two prayers?

"Oh God, I just can't go on anymore! Please, please, please help me. I am desperate to have a better job and someone to love and my life! I will do anything you want if I can just have these things!"

Or, "I am asking for my highest good to have more abundance in my love life, and a warm, inviting environment for my work. I know all is well and perfect in the Universe."

The first one is a desperation prayer, and the second one states clearly what is requested as well as the understanding that everything is as it is supposed to be. This acknowledgment is important because it comes from a place of not only believing but expecting the best outcome. All is well in the Universe, and all is perfect at this moment, even if you are not able to experience it in your current state of energy.

Let's break down the first prayer a bit more so you can understand why this is not as effective as the second one. The first prayer is based on the emotion of desperation and lack. You can feel it, almost taste it, when you read the prayer. Many of us have prayed like this in distressed situations. We're not saying it is wrong to do so. You are human and have human emotions so it is expected to have these moments of not knowing where to turn or for what to ask because of your current state of affairs. Being mindful of your place in the bigger picture will aid greatly in asking for what you truly require instead of what you think you lack. Remember you are a perfect soul, and nothing can change that no matter what happens in your current incarnation. It is important for you to understand this and accept it as your truth because it is here where your foundation is built. Make sure your foundation is built upon strength and the understanding of who you are.

When we ask for love like the first prayer, we're saying "Why am I not lovable and why isn't there anybody to love me?" Maybe you asked for a lesson in having to love yourself before you could feel love from others. This is a common theme on Earth. In order to answer this type of prayer, you would need to be shown ways how the outside world cannot fulfill your need for love. You would have constant reminders of this in the form of abusive relationships, abandonment, and betrayal from those whose love you sought. Again, the lesson is to love yourself so others may love you.

There are so many of you who are unhappy in jobs and this is the second part of this prayer. "Bring me a better job!" I believe everyone has experienced this at one point or another. Maybe you asked for the lesson of sacrifice to make a living at what you enjoy instead of living for money and perceived success. How you respond to your challenges will determine the results. It is not being done to you, so get over it and look for a way to improve your life. This might be accomplished by learning a new trade and actually working in the area of your passion and expertise as opposed to what you fell into to pay the bills.

We understand you believe "money makes the world go round." Would it surprise you to know that money is a lower form of energy in the Universe? I hope you remember from an earlier chapter, but it bears repeating since this money thing has many of you under its control. Money does not make the world go round. Love does. True, heartfelt love. This is not the love you receive from others. It is the love you feel in your heart for yourself and all of humanity as you move through life and experience the glories of planet Earth. This love cannot be bought or sold. It comes from within and once you find it, your life will never be the same. This is what you can ask to receive in abundance. Not money.

We started this chapter talking about your place in the grander scheme and how you are able to ask for additional energy anytime you need. Then we talked about how to ask for it by not asking to replace lack, but to amplify what we already have, which is abundance. Now we need to discuss how to receive this energy.

If you are keeping your tone and frequency at a high level, then receiving this energy will be instantaneous. Ask and ye shall receive[7]. However, if you find there are obstacles in the way of your receiving or you are in a place where you find it difficult to receive, you can change your circumstances to be more in line with us and your Soul Self. Activities as simple as walking in nature, singing a sweet song, meditating, gardening, listening to music, smiling, laughing, putting your awareness into the higher dimensions, and playing with your pet can align your vibration with souls in Heaven.

You may ask, "How do I know if I'm receiving the energy?" Get very quiet, ask for it to come, tune in to your body and observe any changes in energy level or attitude. If you are observant, you will sense the energy coming into your body.

What other things can we bring you? Again, ease and grace in learning your lessons, which will make a tremendous difference in your experiences. You can ask us to show you other scenarios when you are in the middle of making a decision. You might see it as movies in your head. We might show you what it would be like to make a decision one way, then another. Just as when you picked your body, we will not show you everything, but we will give you enough information to make an informed decision. If you are a feeler, you can ask to feel each choice. We can give the feeling of one choice then another. We will never give you the answer outright unless we require you make an immediate change for your highest good. Otherwise, we leave it to your free will by helping you to see and feel what the changes might represent for you. To ask to be shown the differences in your choices, all you need to say is, "Please help me by showing or allowing me to feel what it would be like if this choice was part of my reality." Give us time to give you the information by going into a meditative state, so we can properly give you what you requested.

We are a team—you, your Soul Self, and those of us who are your higher guides. You have to want the best for yourself for us to be able to give it to you, and you have to keep your tone and frequency at a level consistent with your highest good.

You are responsible for your own actions and behaviors. Knowing what you know now, you can never be a victim again. You understand your purpose is to expand your soul by learning the lessons you requested prior to coming into this incarnation, and these lessons are given by the parties you chose, those who agreed to participate in the play. You also understand that you can change the scene and players anytime with your intentional thoughts and prayers. You know how to keep your frequency at a high level to have connection with us and your Soul Self to make this experience the best and most successful one possible.

As I stated before, you are never alone. We cannot emphasize this enough. You now have the tools to ask for the changes required to have a more enriching experience for your time on Earth.

We all have a purpose and reason for being here, whether it is on planet Earth or where I am in Heaven. We are constantly learning. None of us are ever stagnant. In Heaven, we grow and expand intentionally. Where you are, you have the choice to do it intentionally or willy-nilly. Having picked up this book, my guess is you want to live intentionally and figure out your purpose.

There is no secret to the purpose of life on Earth. It is as clear as the lessons you receive and the players you have asked to come into your life. It is where you choose to put your energy and thoughts. It is how you judge others or how you allow others to have their own experiences. It is where you forgive yourself for all the "mistakes" you make and allow yourself to feel our love for you. It is being observant of what your actions do to others and taking responsibility for your life by moving into the energy of abundance and self-acceptance. The purpose of life is to live, love, and write home to tell about it. We love sharing these experiences with you and rejoice when you "get it" or stand up for who you are as a soul. We see the bigger picture for you and do whatever we can to move you in the direction that is for your highest good. We know the hardships you experience as souls in bodies—we have all been there, too, but we realize this is exactly what you requested when you said, "Sign me up for another round!" Most of all, the purpose of life on Earth is to truly live it, taste it, feel it, sink into it, BE it.

There is no other place in the Universe like Earth, and souls are lining up to come onto the planet to experience what you are experiencing right now.

What will you say when you come back home? "I had the time of my life!" or "Darn. I wish I could do that over again." We—your Soul Self, loved ones and me—sure hope it is the first statement. Knowing what you know now, we are certain you will be successful in all you do. Don't ever forget the love and support you have in Heaven or how easy it is to get here. There are no tricks or hoops to jump through. Come out of your body, and you will be here.

Don't try to come earlier than expected, though, because that certainly defeats the purpose.

Never worry. We'll leave the light on for you[8]

CHAPTER FOURTEEN

Questions and Answers

I n this chapter, I will answer questions you sent in via the book website (www.myviewfromHeaven.com) and posts from Facebook (www.facebook.com/myviewfromHeaven).

Val Savidge, Ryan's Mom asks:

Hi J.T., I want you to know you are very loved, and I'm grateful you are able to show your love back to your family and friends still here on Earth. My question is this: Since all of us on Earth have left a portion of our energy in Spirit, you and your Mom and Dad, sister and brother are able to interact with each other where you are. What things do you do together? Do you go exploring together, have picnics etc.?

J.T.: That is a very good question. Because our souls are here in spirit, we do interact with each other. Most of the activities we do together involve assisting those on Earth, but we also enjoy celebrations and feasts. We love to have picnics on other planets; we travel together to these different planets to explore. These planets are usually not like Earth because we like the diversity. You would not believe the different places you can go just using thoughts. This is how we visit you as well, by thinking about you and being there. This is also why it makes sense that when you think of us, we are there right beside you, too.

You touch on a subject I covered in this book and I wanted to make sure the reader truly understands what it means to have a portion of your energy in spirit, and a portion of it in a body on the planet. We have designed it this way to take full advantage of being in a body. Before we enter the body we have chosen, we decide how much energy we will need to complete the tasks we have set out for ourselves. This can range anywhere from 10% to 50%. The remainder of the energy stays in the higher dimensions so your Soul Self in Heaven can assist you on Earth in making the best decisions for your plan. If we brought all of our energy into the incarnations, we may not stay on track. Staying on track is the purpose of the plan. This plan is what you said you would do when you got into your body. It includes the people who you wanted to have come in to support you as your immediate and extended family, friends, adversaries, and all other players. It also contains the scenarios you wanted to run to learn your lessons. These could be lessons you did not complete in previous lifetimes, or important new lessons for you to understand, not only for yourself, but for the rest of humanity.

Your question also asked about what we do as souls while our incarnations are on Earth. We do enjoy being with each other, hence we create the multiple lifetimes together on the planet. There's much to learn and do in Heaven, and no limits to where we can go and what we can experience. Believe me, we take full advantage of this. We love celebrations on Earth and in Heaven. You can count on the fact your loved one is celebrating something, anything at any given time.

Danyilla asks:
Is every child greeted and guided where to go when their bodies die? Do they always know where to go so they are safe and taken care of? How can parents/families know their child/loved ones are happy and safe on the other side?

J.T.: Yes, every child is greeted and guided where to go when his or her body stops working. Your loved ones are visited prior to their passing, so they are not afraid when the time comes. Whoever visits informs them of what is going to happen and who will be there when the child comes out of the body. In the first chapter of this book, I wrote about Hope. Hope was the soul who told me what was happening and what to expect. She kept me calm and informed. She let me know my parents would be fine and that I would be able to help them in special ways.

For anyone reading this book who has had to say goodbye to a child, please know they are in Heaven with me and safe. Children who pass are very experienced at leaving their bodies and usually do not have any issues finding their way. Most of us remember what it is like to be in this energy form as soon as our soul leaves the body because we have not been in our bodies as long. We have plenty of help from relatives who have passed and those who are close to us in spirit. Even if we never met the relative who comes to help when we leave, we know him or her from spirit. I knew my Grandfather Roger and my Grandmother Bernice by their energy, even though as J.T. I never met them on planet Earth.

There are many ways to know your child is safe and happy. The best method is to ask them. My mom has been teaching bereaved parents how to connect and communicate with their children for many years. You can start this process with her book, *A Bridge to Healing: J.T.'s Story Companion Workbook.* It has many exercises to teach you this communication. Your child, I can guarantee, has already given you signs and messages, even if you haven't been able to experience them. There is no exception to this. Children always send signs and messages. Sometimes it is very difficult for parents to receive them because of the grief or guilt around the child's passing. Working through the grief, guilt, anger, resentment, etc., is a great way to start the process of being able to receive from your child.

Please do not misunderstand me. I am not saying it is an easy task, or that you just get over the grief because that is not how it works on Earth. But you can process much of what you experience emotionally to open up and sense the signs and messages from your child.

KW asks:

Do we make soul contracts with other beings who meet us here in human form to fulfill a purpose? Are there any intuitive indicators we can look for to help us understand the nature of these planned "meetings"?

J.T.: Yes, we do make soul contracts with others who meet us in human form to fulfill many purposes. Most of our encounters with other life forms on the planet take place because of the soul contracts and what we said we wanted to learn.

I want to talk a little bit about soul contracts and lessons because they are very intricate and often misunderstood. A soul contract is an agreement you made before entering your current incarnation and body because you said you wanted to accomplish something specific. Soul contracts usually involve multiple souls because we need the assistance in getting done what we want to get done. Sometimes, players are changed in the middle of the plan, and this can throw us off because we believe we had a soul contract with that particular person to stay with us and help us get where we needed to go. The truth is there are multiple souls on the planet at any given time who can step in and assist us, maybe in a better way than the original player. An example of where change might be needed is if the player asserts his or her free will and, in that process, the player does not support you in what you need to get done. In this case, the contract between you and that player is altered, and there will be other ways that player will assist you. The next player will step in and continue the plan. I talk about this example because it happens more frequently than you may realize. It does not mean that person failed you, because they will teach you something different about yourself. We work diligently here to keep all the players in alignment with the goals, but honestly, the scenarios move rapidly and changes do need to be implemented to keep everyone on track. It is quite possible you have a soul contract with someone who has said they wanted to assist in a certain aspect of your life, but then they get to Earth and cannot fulfill that contract. This is absolutely fine and we make other arrangements.

Everyone in your life has come in for a purpose, of course. To identify what that purpose might be, you can tune in and ask your Soul Self. We all have the ability to do this. One of the things that might be an intuitive indicator, as you phrased it, is the knowing-ness of the person, even though you just met him or her. The person feels familiar, as if you have known this person for years. Well, you have, which is why you feel this way. Any time there is a connection between two souls, it is because there is a connection here where I am. If you are observant, you will know immediately this person is in your life to fulfill a contract.

Emily S. asks:
I would like to know how our relationships with our loved ones change after we die. My husband and I are in love now in this life, but will that change on the other side? The possibility of our love and relationship changing scares me a little - I really would like to be with him forever.

J.T.: The question you ask is an important one, and I'm sure many of the readers wonder about this. Yes, you will be with him, or his Soul Self, for as long as you both choose. You are part of the same soul family and enjoy being together in Heaven, as well as on Earth, so trust me when I say that relationship will not only continue, but will change in ways you may not understand right now because it is very different here. We relate to each other in Heaven as energy which is much more powerful than when you're in a physical body. More than likely, your relationship will surpass its current intensity.

We have many "soul mates," as you call them on Earth, and given this, you have many opportunities to feel that incredible connection with more than just one person. Because our soul families are fairly large, never think there is only one person in the Universe for you. I say this so you all understand the closeness you can have with other souls on your planet. These do not need to be romantic connections, but soul connections. It is very critical to remember this.

Lara K. and Linda A. ask:
Do you reconnect with your loved ones who had already passed?

J.T.: Absolutely! After I left, I was greeted by my grandparents who had passed. Those in Heaven cannot wait to greet you when you come home. As souls, we look forward to these reunions. We will welcome you with love and open arms, even if our relationship with you was rocky on the planet, or we left with unspoken words or apologies. We will be waiting for you. We love to greet our loved ones and show you the ropes. You will remember what it is like to be home, and we will enjoy reminiscing about our lifetime together. You still have many things to accomplish in your current incarnations, and there is no rushing this process. Do your best to learn all the lessons you asked to learn and experience life in incredible ways. You can bet we will see each other again.

Paul K. asks:
I lost my grandmother in the Big Thompson flood in 1976 and they never did find her body. Grandma, where are you and is all ok?

J.T.: I can assure you and others in similar situations that your loved ones are with me here in Heaven. There is always purpose to passings, no matter how traumatic or devastating. I know your grandmother visits you often, as do others' loved ones. It is one of the ways we can assure you we are doing fine. No matter what has happened to our human form at the end of that lifetime, please understand the soul can never be harmed or destroyed in any way.

One of the ways you can find out how your grandmother is doing is by asking her. Get quiet and ask her to come and give you the sense she is there with you. Everyone can do this. Everyone has the ability to connect with us in Heaven. Sometimes people expect to have very obvious signs from loved ones, but often it is very subtle and we need to be observant.

Linda A. asks:
Is it all I hope it is?

J.T.: It is all you hope it is and so much more. In Heaven, the strife and challenges you have faced disappear. They melt away as your soul leaves your body and you return to your true form. Again, there is much for you to do in your current incarnations, so there's no need to rush to get here. You will get here exactly when you said you wanted to come home. I promise you it is more beautiful than the human mind can comprehend.

Mary S. asks:
Have you seen Elvis?

J.T.: This is a funny question. We've heard your jokes about Elvis and laughed with you. I want to say something about celebrities who pass. Of course, they are like everybody else who passes and transitions into energy. Because their lives were very public, many of the celebrities who pass tend to stay close to the Earth for a little longer to look at the impact they had on the planet. This is almost like part of their life review, but they get to see it from a different perspective. All souls who have been in bodies on Earth have a permanent imprint of energy here in Heaven. This means you can connect with anyone at anytime, should you so desire. Yes, I have seen Elvis. I've also seen Isaac Newton, Beethoven, Jesus, and Lord Dunraven, to name a few. They are a little different here than when they were on the planet.

Mandy asks:
Are you ok up in Heaven, & know I love and miss you so very much?

J.T: I am okay here in Heaven! Actually, more than okay because I get to see you and my loved ones in a very different way, and participate in your lives more than if I was still in a body. We do know you miss and love us, and we miss you and love you beyond words. You can always talk to me, any time. That goes for all of your loved ones. I will answer every time you ask a question.

Lara K asks:
Does everyone go to Heaven?

J.T.: Everyone who wants to go to Heaven goes to Heaven. Heaven is a state of energy, and anyone can achieve this state. Some choose to arrive at that state of energy more quickly than others. We're all given the opportunity and the information to change our state of energy to be at the level of energy where I am. There are many choices souls can make after they leave an incarnation. Some choose to follow their belief system which may incorporate an in-between state of energy because they do not feel or understand they can go to Heaven immediately. For the same reasons, others choose to stay in the state of energy when they leave their bodies because they feel or believe they will not be welcome in Heaven. This is absolutely false because everyone is welcome in this state of energy. It is where we begin our journey into bodies, and where we end our journey from a body.

There is no rush to get here and each soul must decide where they want to be energetically.

Maureen W. asks:
Do souls reincarnate?

J.T.: Many souls have reincarnated, and many have not. It is up to the soul to decide which lessons need to be repeated, or what new learning can be achieved in a new incarnation. We have an immense learning system at certain levels of energy in Heaven. You can go to a different level and learn just as you would in a school on Earth. Usually, after we have returned from an incarnation, we take time to evaluate what we might want to experience next. Because Earth has such a unique way of teaching lessons, many choose to come back into another form. It is rather invigorating when we choose our lifetimes together. We are very excited about the prospect of being in physical form and sharing experiences.

For others, one lifetime is enough and they choose to return to their place of origin, or they may hang out in whatever state of energy they pick to learn and understand more about the human spirit in our Energy System. Because we have so many souls from other places in the Universe helping us right now, many will return to their own planets and Energy Systems after they are done with their incarnations.

Elizabeth V. asks:
Are you happy?

J.T.: What makes me happy is seeing the light and love many of you are experiencing on the planet right now. If you could see this from my perspective, you would be smiling, also. All of your bright lights shining upward to the Heavens indicate the success for which we are all striving is being accomplished in amazing ways on your planet. My hope is more people pay attention to the light and love, instead of the perceived darkness and hatred. Notice how I said perceived because it is not real. Love is real and certainly the light is real. This is what makes me happy.

Judy L. asks:

Do you know my daughter? If so, do you hang out with her or do souls even hang out with each other there?

J.T.: In this particular case, I do know your daughter because you and my mom know each other. Since we are all one soul truly, on that level we do all know each other. The more important piece of this to understand is who we are at the soul level because our incarnations are just one fragment of our energy. Again, this does not mean you can't contact that fragment because you can at anytime. It does mean that once we get back here, we join with the many other pieces of our soul to become that much greater energy, our Soul Self. We do hang out with our soul family here and experience a very different kind of life. Many of us are busy helping other souls come back into the energy form, teaching about the way things work on planet Earth so new souls going in have a better understanding of what they will endure, and of course, creating on Earth and other planets. This is my favorite part of being in energy form.

Diana L. asks:
Do you have 'tasks' - similar to our work or can you choose your own?

J.T.: Yes, we have tasks as I mentioned above. We do choose our projects and we all have specialties. Sometimes these specialties change depending on what our soul wants to accomplish. A good example of this is specialty guides. I have been a specialty guide for others on planet Earth. What these guides do is come in to assist a human with a particular task or experience. A specialty guide could be someone to aid you in getting a new job in a different field, one that is closer to what you said you wanted to experience in your life plan. Another task a specialty guide could have is to teach you a new skill. Sometimes when we are not able to accomplish something we wanted to on Earth, such as getting a doctorate degree, so we decide to assist someone else in getting that degree. When we help you in this manner, we grow with you. It is almost as if we get that degree for ourselves and experience it vicariously through you.

Natasha I. asks:

How does free will work? We come here with a plan, can we change it? For example, dying young or suffering from an illness. Are we the creators of our lives?

J.T.: Free will is the reason so many energies line up to get into bodies on your planet. It is such a gift to have free will. It works like this: we decide before we come into a body what we want to learn and roughly how we want to learn it. We're not given many details about the experience since this would ruin the whole point of the exercise, which is to learn. We are given some information and then we get to decide how it looks. We choose our partners, our parents, and our siblings, and how each of them will interact with the experience we wish to receive. We all agree on our parts of the play and, basically, how it will work. What we don't know are the specifics, which is the exciting part because this is where our free will defines how it is done. Life is like a web with many branches and twists and turns. If we go one way on the web, then we encounter the people and the circumstances set forth on that part of the web which is designed specifically for our learning. If we choose a different way to go, the circumstances and people might be different, but the lesson will be the same. Sometimes when we go a certain way, we veer a little more off course than what our Soul Selves want for us, and life gets difficult.

Whenever there is difficulty in your life, you must ask, "Am I on course?" Sometimes, the difficulty will be on any part of the web because this is the experience you wanted to create. Other times, the difficulty is because you are not learning or might be stuck, and your Soul Self wants to unstick you. Sometimes this is done by harshness to get your attention. How do you know if you chose a difficult path, or are on a difficult path and need to change course? Check into your heart and feel your way through it.

The heart is an amazing, incredible energy field created to guide you and assist in decision-making and path choosing. Sometimes our heart is wounded, so decisions are coming from that wounded place. This needs to be healed so the heart can once again be our lighthouse. Science shows that the electromagnetic field around the heart is much greater than that around our brains. This is not a fluke. This is so you will be guided by your heart in making decisions for your highest good.

To answer your question on whether we're able to change the plan once in body, such as altering when and how we pass, there are definitely options we include in our plan to allow for changes we make on the planet.

For me, I did not want to pass from a long illness because I had already done that in other lifetimes, so I chose to leave by a quick ailment. There were three times I could have left the incarnation of J.T.—the first time was when I was four and I got croup. My throat closed up and was cutting off my air supply. I chose not to go at that time because of circumstances with my family. The second time I could have left was in 2006 when a parasite infected my throat. Again, I chose to stay because of family circumstances. When I did leave in March 2007, it was my last exit option, and I chose to leave from the flu, which really was about my air supply again being cut off. All of these instances involved my throat, which is how I chose to leave that incarnation.

Sometimes we do make changes in the plan to accommodate circumstances. The way in which we pass is always another opportunity to learn about human form.

You are the creator of your life, rather, co-creator because your incarnation is only a small piece of who you are. We always say in Heaven, you can create anything in life that is for your highest good. Sometimes from an earthly perspective, you cannot see what is for your highest good, and therefore, you must defer to your Soul Self. The more you are in line with your highest good and your Soul Self, the faster your creations come to form.

Jo U. asks:
I have been asked to ask you what is a day like for you. What kind of things do you do when you are not supporting us here on Earth?

J.T.: I do many things during your Earth day. My main focus these days is to support Earth's energy by holding her energy within my own. Many of us are doing this now so the planet has a better opportunity to support all of you. I also enjoy creating on other planets and learning from other systems of energy so I can teach about the systems to all of you. We do not have days or nights where I am because there is no time or space here. This is a hard concept for many of you to understand. Don't worry, because it is not something you need to master while you are on Earth.

A.S. asks:
How much of our personality comes with us to Earth? How much of other aspects of our Soul Self comes with us?

J.T.: This is a wonderful question because we do have individual personalities here, and we love to bring these in to our incarnations on Earth. As you learn about your other incarnations, you may see a theme emerging. We also have incarnations contrary to our preferred demeanor because how else would we learn about different aspects of us? Many times, though, we bring in the personality traits we enjoy from lifetime to lifetime. Let me say, we all have a wicked sense of humor here. This might be surprising to those who believe in a certain type of Heaven. We enjoy laughing and joking around. There are some, such as certain members of your Council, who may appear more solemn. There is purpose in this since you may need to take things more seriously in your life.

We can bring as much of our Soul Self personality as we wish. Many times we will bring in our specialties, such as engineering, teaching, nursing, and the like. If these are our specialties in Heaven, we may want to have similar professions in the lifetimes we create. This is because we feel most comfortable in these professions. There are times we are not able to experience our specialties during our incarnations, and choose to guide others after we have returned to our Soul Selves.

Sue V. asks:
Once we pass over do we get to know and understand the things that eluded us while we were on Earth?

J.T.: We all have that "a-ha" moment when we do our life review and see where we may have missed the point of an exercise. We do not understand everything from all perspectives, because in order to do this we must experience it as souls.

We all have the opportunity to change and enhance who we are by the learning we do in spirit and bodies. If as souls we got to see everything and have the answers, we would never go back into bodies because there would be no point. It is like a grand-size science experiment with cause, effect, and unexpected results. We love to see things from all perspectives here, as it gives us a better understanding of how to operate in the dense environment of Earth.

We know and understand much more once we return to our Soul Selves, but there is always more to learn.

Michelle H. asks:
I would like to know if you still experience the range of emotions in Heaven, such as anger, sorrow, happiness and so on?

J.T.: The intenseness of the emotions you experience on Earth does not transfer to Heaven. We see and feel your experiences from a detached perspective. Love is always part of who we are, regardless of our energetic state. The emotions on the planet were created for your earthly experiences and learning from each other in circumstances created for a lifetime. We do have happiness and joy here because these are part of love. We do not have disappointment because there's nothing to be disappointed about. Everything you do in your bodies is for a purpose, and we see it all as a way for you to understand who you are. Many on your planet believe their loved ones in Heaven might be dissatisfied or angry with choices they have made in their lives. This is not the case. We see what is for your highest good, but we are not upset if you choose to go a different direction because we understand you will still learn what is needed, even though the lessons might be harsher. We do not roll over in our graves, so please don't worry about how we perceive your choices.

Stephanie J. asks:

I imagine that we can be pure energy just being or we can create physical type places and participate in Earth type activities. Is that true that we can do both or is it just one or the other? Is it anything like the character "Q" from Star Trek? Is our Earth existence like being hooked up to a virtual realty interface only not knowing it? (another Star Trek reference). Is our energy now in a bubble created to support time and you are outside this bubble of time?

J.T.: Yes, we can do both at the same time. We can be pure energy and create an Earth-like environment for our enjoyment simultaneously. I would say the character Q is a rather finite character and does not describe what we do or who we are as energy forms. Great character, though!

You ask another great question about the virtual reality interface. There is a similarity to what we do and the virtual reality games. However, it is more like those of us in spirit are observing the part of us that is participating with a virtual reality console. Let's say we have this window we look through to see the part of our energy in a body, almost like we're watching a movie. We are observing, perhaps influencing, as part of us is interacting. This is how it is different than a virtual reality interface.

The time bubble, as you put it, is created for the distinct purpose of limiting what you experience in a particular incarnation. We do not use the concept of time in Heaven. We see everything happening at once, not on the time-space continuum. This gives us a distinct perspective to assist you in the best way possible, given all outcomes your soul desires. It is an extraordinary model, and is so much more intricate than what I can describe here. Suffice it to say, you are all amazing beings in very unique existences, and your Soul Selves guide you every step of the way.

Mechelle L. asks:
Is there sadness in Heaven? When a child leaves Earth but wants to stay are they allowed to replace a parental guide from the other side?

J.T.: We do not have the emotion of sadness in Heaven. It is reserved for those on planet Earth. We see you and all of your experiences from the perspective of learning and understanding. We have the ability to put ourselves in your shoes to comprehend why you experience the emotions you do, but it is not the same as having those feelings ourselves.

When a child leaves an incarnation, there is always a plan. No one leaves an incarnation unless they have chosen to do so. This choice is from the Soul Self, and all of those who are involved have agreed to this experience from the soul perspective. This is a hard concept for many parents to understand because it sounds preposterous that we would choose the heartache and agony of losing a child. If you read the other parts of this book, it will better explain why we make these choices and what we expect to gain from them. Children who leave their bodies at early ages are not new to this experience. They are well versed in how to raise their tone and frequency to get to the higher levels like where I am. Because the parents have asked for the experience of losing a child, the child's soul is very often a primary guide for one or both parents. The Soul Self knows the connection between parent and child is extraordinary, and uses that connection to guide and assist those still in bodies who are affected by that soul's departure. It is a guarantee to anyone who has lost a child that the child's soul is right beside you as you are reading this. There are no exceptions to this.

Kristi U. asks:

When a child passes as an infant/newborn do they continue to grow and interact with us? My sister passed shortly after birth over 40 years ago and recently I have felt a strong connection and need to know if it is her. Do families reconnect in Heaven- grandparents, siblings, etc.?

J.T.: This question has two answers. The first the answer is yes, we continue to grow and interact with you as the age you would expect. The other answer is no, we may come to you as older or younger depending on the circumstances. Let me explain. We can come to you as any age, and we usually choose either an age you would expect or need, or one we want you to experience. An example of this is when I came to the medium on stage when my parents were in the audience. I came to her as a teenager because I wanted her to take me seriously. I come to my mother as the seven year old who left, the fifteen year old I would be today, my Soul Self which is ageless, or the wise older soul when she needs a push to take things a little more seriously. Your sister would come as her current age because you would be able to relate to her more than if she came as an infant. Here in Heaven, we have no age, although our Soul Selves can be seen aged between twenty and thirty years old from your perspective. This is only because you need a physical form to understand. Many see us as the pure energy we are instead of in a physical form. We truly can take any form we choose. It does not have to be human, although coming as human is best for you since you may not understand us if we came in a different form.

Yes, families do reconnect when they return to soul form.

Michelle H. asks:
If you had a handicap here on Earth does that go away when you go to Heaven? Do you stay the same age?

J.T.: Absolutely, we do not have handicaps in Heaven. Such issues are always a part of the soul contract so the soul can experience a different form of existence. Those who choose handicaps are definitely older souls. They would not have made the choice to have dysfunctions unless they were very experienced in coming to planet Earth.

These maladies do not transfer to the Soul Self. It is part of our physical form which we release when the soul leaves the body. Some may hold onto the physical illness until they understand they no longer need this, and by releasing the physical malady, they can increase their tone and frequency to get to the higher levels.

As I answered in the last question, we do not have age in Heaven. We can come to you as any age. Our souls are ageless because there is no time where we are.

Andi B. asks:
Are you still a child over there? Do you age? If you are still a child what do you do? Is there anybody taking care of you, teaching you?

J.T.: I kept these questions about our age here as separate questions because, obviously, there is a theme here. Many of you are concerned or wonder about this. I hope through this book and this Q&A you understand more about how energy works in Heaven. We do not have age here because we do not have time or space. We are pure energy. We do not require anyone to take care of us, although we do have many teachers who share information and knowledge. These are extraordinary souls who have been to Earth countless times and have lived many iterations of life. They share their understanding of what they have learned with all of us. To truly understand, firsthand experience is required. If we want to really get it, we put this request into our next incarnation so we can experience it ourselves.

Deborah M. asks:

Since the Sun, stars, planets, etc., are in our "reality"...do they exist in Heaven, or were they created for our experience here on Earth? If they do not...what does Heaven "look like"?

J.T.: This question also has two answers. Because we are part of your reality we have created together, the stars, sun, and planets are also part of the reality here in Heaven. We all are the suns, stars, and planets, and we have a personal relationship with all of them. If you recall in an earlier chapter, I talked about Earth and how she has a soul. All planets, stars and our sun have souls which come from the Universal Source of energy. We are all part of this Universal Source so we are all part of the celestial beings. You can say we have dual lives. Again, part of us is holding the energy for the Earth and the entire Energy System, and part of us is in pure energy.

Heaven looks like whatever we're thinking about because our thoughts become instant reality. If we think of lush green fields, then Heaven becomes lush green fields. If we think about fire, then Heaven becomes fire. In this case, fire cannot hurt us.

We are all creators, in Heaven and in bodies. Earth and Heaven are manifestations of our thoughts and dreams—a great reminder to watch your thoughts. What are you creating? Beauty and joy, or despair and fear? The choice is always yours.

EPILOGUE

You are now smarter than the average bear, and for that matter, the average human. This is not like one of those books you finish and put on your bookshelf, forgetting the content of what you read. This life-changing book provides the impetus to make your experience on this planet the most exciting and rewarding possible. This is not the kind of book you read once and believe you have all of the materials assimilated in your brain. The concepts we discussed are beyond much of the information you may receive in the mainstream, regardless of your spiritual practice. I recommend reading this book more than once. Each time you will receive a new message through the words on the page and visits from me and your other helpers as you are reading it. For everyone who picks up this book and dedicates the time and energy to consider it with intent, you have special guides now to assist you on your new journey, an *informed* journey. No longer can you hide in the closet and pretend you don't understand why you are here, or what you can do to make your life better. Reflection on what you have learned is crucial to a better understanding of the purpose of your life.

I am grateful to you for receiving these words into your heart and mind because without you, there would be no us.

You must understand now you are much more than the flesh and blood created as your human suit. This book only touched the surface of where I am and what it means to be a soul, and to have life on Earth. I encourage you to keep studying your new paradigm with those whom you trust and those who have shown themselves to be reliable sources. You are your own psychic barometer. Tune in to your body and soul when making decisions about teachers, guides, confidants, partners, and the like, because you have inside knowledge now on what it all means and your part in this marvelous play.

Beware false prophets. Always trust your inner knowing. I say this now because you have opened up to so many possibilities after reading this book, that it is possible those around you will sense you are different. Don't be surprised if more spiritual people want to be around you. The energy shift you make will reflect this. Others may wish to be in your presence, which is fine as long as they do not drain your energy.

The point is, you are a new person in this instant and with that, comes fresh responsibility for your life. You have an action plan, or will soon, on how you want to change things according to what you read in this book. Don't underestimate yourself or your capabilities. If you get nothing else from this book, this is what I want you to know: *You are far more than what you have been led to believe.*

I will continue to channel with my mom and give her information about any changes that need to be made in your lives based upon changes in Heaven and the plan we all agreed to. This is an exciting time for our Universe and it is meant to be shared and experienced to the highest possible degree with love, joy, understanding of each other, and knowing we are One. Each thing you do on Earth, we feel here. Observe your thoughts and actions. Feel from your heart with love and acceptance for everyone. You are the light that shines so brightly. We see your brilliance and honor you for your participation in this adventure.

Whenever there is a question about your part in this play, ask us for assistance, and we will do anything we can to bring you the information.

**Stay open to us.
Life does not have to be
hard. It just needs to be
lived. I thank you for all
you do.**

POSTCRIPT

By Sarina Baptista

Writing this book with J.T. was an amazing experience. When I began my communication with him, I just wanted to know he was safe and okay. I had no idea I would witness such a mastermind. I did not know at the time who J.T. really was, or what contracts our souls had made. All I knew was that he was my son and I wanted to talk to him and keep the relationship we had on Earth.

Boy, was I in for a surprise.

When we first started communicating as guide and student, J.T. told me things I could hardly believe. I was only a beginner at mediumship and thought surely, I was not understanding him correctly. Over the last seven years, I have received instructions from J.T., and now I know our connection is clear and strong. I have no doubt about who he is, his role in my life, and the lives of humankind. If I think about it too much, I get overwhelmed because of the grandness of his spirit.

When we were writing the first book (*A Bridge to Healing: J.T.'s Story – A Mother's Grief Journey and Return to Hope*) and I had to go through the details of his death, it was excruciating. To boot, my editor said I had to rewrite the first chapter because it was too choppy, so I had to relive J.T.'s passing over and over again with the words I was writing on my computer. Imagine my hesitation when J.T. and I began this book, and here we were again talking about how he left his incarnation. Regardless, I knew this book had to be written, so I sucked it up and began to channel my son's words.

I started by typing what J.T. told me into a document. It was painstakingly slow, so he encouraged me to dictate the words into my phone's voice recorder, which converts the spoken words into a computer file. That is, until my phone began to crash as I channeled. My eyes were closed while J.T. communicated, so I did not know the recording stopped until I opened my eyes. By then much of his words were lost.

I asked for assistance and the solution came in the form of a new computer which had a factory installed speech recognition program. I no longer needed the phone recorder, and the frustration of losing the channeled information from J.T. was eliminated. When you're working with the heavenly realm, always be open to possibilities because you will receive answers to your questions, as long as you request the help.

At first I thought I needed to have complete silence, be in a perfect state of high vibration after at least a half hour meditation in order to channel my son. I realized if I waited for everything to align, this book would never get done. Fortunately, the relationship I now have with J.T. is one that he is part of me and I am part of him, so channeling is as easy as talking to myself.

Among different kinds of channeling, there is one where the person's consciousness leaves the body and allows the energies being channeled to enter the body and speak through him or her. I did this form of channeling a few years ago, but had a difficult time staying out of my body while they were occupying it. It was not that I didn't trust these energies because they were from much higher dimensions and wanted to teach us about healing. It was because I did not like to give up control and be away from my body.

To write this book, I did another kind of channeling with J.T.; I allowed him to talk through me but in a way where I was present and aware of what I was doing. Instead of hearing the words and having the conversation with him in my head as I usually do, I dictated the communications into the computer. It was very simple to do.

One exercise I have my psychic students practice is a form of automatic writing, where they do what I did with J.T. for this book. I learned this technique in the beginning of my psychic training, and it is extremely effective to connect with guides, angels and loved ones on the other side. Sit at a computer and say a prayer of intention and protection. Then invite that angel, guide or loved one to talk with you. Close your eyes and type out everything you hear.

I include this little piece of training because it is how I was able to communicate with my son, and it led to writing this incredible book.

Life can get busy and others' priorities end up trumping our own. We cannot allow this to happen any longer. We need to be the priority now. If I can do this work, grieve the loss of a son, home school my other children, and see a full load of clients, then maybe you can make the changes J.T. suggests so you can lead a more guided life. If I can have this connection with J.T., there is nothing stopping you from developing yours with those in Heaven. They see the best for you, and want to help you reach where you need to go.

I appreciate your openness to the information J.T. has presented, and if there is any way I can assist you in fulfilling your goals, please do not hesitate to ask.

Namaste and many blessings.

Sarina Baptista

ACKNOWLEDGMENTS

There are so many people we wish to acknowledge for their help, guidance, love, and understanding through this process. First and foremost, we wish to acknowledge our family—John, Lacey and Anthony. Through thick and thin, you have believed in us, supported us, and held down the fort as we worked on this book. Thank you!

To those on this journey, incredible souls and dear friends (in alphabetical order): Angeline Jackson, Becky Ellsworth, Donna Visocky, Elizabeth Vann, Faith Rodriguez, Jaime Parrott, Jackie Mihalchick, Jo Underwood, Joanie DeLaGarza, John Holland, Jonelle Davis, Katie Cashman, Lisa and Kevin White, Mike, Kari and Emily Sever, Monika Buerger, Scott James, Susan Beber, Suzanne Giesemann, Terrie Baney—thank you for shining your light so others will find their way.

To those who knew J.T. and are still in our lives: Margaret Rado, Denise Regelman, Jennifer Padrta, Kari Weiler, Kate Klusman, Karen Hawkwood—the J.T. Fan Club. Thank you for believing in us and supporting us through the good, the bad, and the crazy.

To our incredible editor, Sue Wang. You are truly remarkable and we could not have published this without your assistance.

To all of our clients who have pushed us beyond the limitations of our beliefs and into the realm of the Twilight Zone, thank you for trusting us.

ABOUT THE AUTHORS

J T Baptista was born Joseph Tracy Baptista in October 1999 in Northern California. His early years of schooling were at Valley Montessori School in Livermore, CA, where he demonstrated the essence of his spirit. A new student entered his class mid-year, scared and visibly upset. J.T. was only three years old, but he understood his classmate needed comforting. He got up, grabbed a tissue, sat down with the boy and gave him a hug and the tissue. They became best friends, and remained close until J.T's passing.

When his family moved to Northern Colorado in June 2005, J.T. was only five years old and had fears about leaving his old friends, but with his warm, caring and fun personality, he quickly made many friends. Two hundred people, adults and children alike, attended J.T.'s funeral in April 2007. He had been taking Karate, and the Karate school students honored him by attending the funeral in their white uniforms, *Gi's*. J.T. was buried in his *Gi* and given an honorary black belt, which the school Sensei himself put as J.T. lay in his casket. During the ceremony, the officiant asked if anyone wished to say something. Child after child stood up and said, "J.T. was my best friend," and proceeded to tell us about all of the wonderful things he did for them and others.

In his short seven years on this planet, J.T. made an impression wherever he went. He loved NASCAR, playing with his matchbox cars, riding his scooter, going shooting with his dad, and hanging out with his family.

On March 30, 2007, J.T.'s body stopped working due to complications from the flu.

He continues his work of spreading love and joy from Heaven now. J.T. spends his time assisting all forms of energy on Earth and in other places in theUniverse.

Sarina Baptista is an internationally-renowned Speaker, Author, Spiritual Teacher, and Psychic Medium. She was a featured speaker for the "Life, Death and Beyond" International Conference in Crete, Greece, and is the resident psychic for Clear Channel's Big Country 97.9FM in Northern Colorado. Her clients include adults and children from Australia, Canada, Italy, India, the UK, Saudi Arabia, and the USA. Her purpose is to connect us to our angels, guides and loved ones, and teach us how to access this information. She discovered her gifts through her own tragedy—the passing of her seven-year-old son, J.T., in March 2007. She learned her son did not really die; he was still very close, leading her to her mediumship gifts so she could help other bereaved parents connect with their children who have passed, as well as teach everyday people how to access their own Divine Guidance in everything they do.

Sarina works with a collective of Guides who sees what her clients need and assists in each session. She has created several mediumship training programs, including one-on-one mediumship mentoring, long distance training, workshops and webinars to teach how to connect with the other side based on what she has learned from J.T. and the Guides. She holds monthly live events and development workshops demonstrating how we are all connected.

Sarina is also the Psychic Investigator Team Lead for Third Eye Paranormal Investigators, a Northern Colorado paranormal team, and educates home and business owners about these "residents" in their space. For more information on Sarina, please visit www.sarinabaptista.com.

RESOURCES

Below are resources for the reader to explore more about this subject matter and the concepts of life after death.

Books

Proof of Heaven, by Eben Alexander, M.D. (Simon and Schuster, 2012)
Power of the Soul, by John Holland (Hay House 2007)
Many Lives, Many Masters, by Brian L. Weiss, M.D. (Fireside 1988)
Journey of Souls, by Michael Newton, Ph.D. (Llewellyn 1994)
Wolf's Message, by Suzanne Giesemann (Waterside Productions 2014)
Ask and It Is Given, by Esther and Jerry Hicks (Hay House 2004)
The Spontaneous Healing of Belief, by Gregg Braden (Hay House 2008)

Websites

Bridge to Healing – Sarina Baptista
www.sarinabaptista.com

John Holland, Psychic Medium
www.johnholland.com

Eben Alexander
www.ebenalexander.com

BellaSpark Productions
bellaspark.com

ENDNOTES

[1] *Power of the Soul*, by John Holland (Hay House 2007)

[2] *Journey of Souls*, by Michael Newton, Ph.D. (Llewellyn 1994)

[3] *The Secret*, by Rhonda Byrne (Atria Books/Beyond Words 2010)

[4] The Movie *Contact* is a 1997 American science fiction drama film directed by Robert Zemeckis. It is a film adaptation of Carl Sagan's 1985 novel of the same name; Sagan and his wife Ann Druyan wrote the story outline for the film.

[5] The original *Star Trek* series focuses on the 23rd century adventures of Captain James T. Kirk and the U.S.S. Enterprise. Created by Gene Roddenberry, the science fiction television series starred William Shatner as Captain Kirk, Leonard Nimoy as Mr. Spock, and DeForest Kelley as Dr. Leonard "Bones" McCoy aboard the fictional Federation starship USS Enterprise. The series originally aired in 1966

[6] Shakespeare, William. *As You Like It*, Act II, Scene VII, line 139-40, 1623.

[7] *English Standard Version Bible*. Matthew 7.7-8 "Ask, and it will be given to you; seek, and you will find; knock, and it will be opened to you. For everyone who asks receives, and the one who seeks finds, and to the one who knocks it will be opened."

[8] Motel 6. Advertising tagline, 1986

18660999R00102

Printed in Great Britain
by Amazon